SolidWorks 2015
Learn by doing

Tutorial Books

Limit of Liability/Disclaimer of Warranty:

Trademarks:

Table of Contents

INTRODUCTION

SolidWorks is a package adding a great value to enterprises. It offers a set of tools, which are easy-to-use to design, document and simulate 3D models. Using this software, you can speed up the design process and reduce the product development costs.

This book provides a systematic approach for users to learn SolidWorks. It is aimed at new SolidWorks users. However, users of previous versions of SolidWorks may also find this book useful for them to learn the new enhancements. This book guides the user from starting a SolidWorks 2015 session to constructing parts, assemblies, and drawings. Each chapter has components explained with the help of real world models.

Scope of this book

If you are a student or engineer who is interested to learn SolidWorks 2015 for mechanical design, then this book helps you to do it easily and quickly. You will also enjoy the learning process by creating real world models. In addition, if you are a graphical learner, then you will find this book very interesting.

The topics in this book include Getting Started with SolidWorks 2015, Basic Part Modeling, Creating Assemblies, Creating Drawings, Additional Modeling Tools, and Sheet Metal Modeling.

Chapter 1 introduces SolidWorks. The user interface and terminology are discussed in this chapter.

Chapter 2 takes you through the creation of your first SolidWorks model. You create simple parts.

Chapter 3 teaches you to create assemblies. It explains the Top-down and Bottom-up approaches for designing an assembly. You create an assembly using the Bottom-up approach.

Chapter 4 teaches you to create drawings of the models created in the earlier chapters. You will also learn to place exploded views, and part list of an assembly.

Chapter 5: In this chapter, you will learn sketch tools.

Chapter 6: In this chapter, you will learn additional modeling tools to create complex models.

Chapter 7: introduces you to Sheet Metal modeling. You will create a sheet metal part using the tools available in the Sheet Metal environment.

Chapter 8: In this chapter, you will learn to create assemblies using Top-down approach and apply some advanced mates.

Chapter 9: In this chapter, you will learn to add annotations to drawings.

Chapter 10: In this chapter, you will learn Surface Modeling tools.

Chapter11: This chapter introduces you Mold design.

Chapter 12: In this chapter, you will learn to create Weldments.

Chapter 13: In this chapter, you will learn DimXpert tools.

Chapter 14: This chapter introduces you to Appearances and Rendering.

Chapter 1: Getting Started

In this chapter, you will learn some of the most commonly used features of SolidWorks. In addition, you will learn about the user interface.

SolidWorks is a parametric and feature-based system that allows you to create 3D parts, assemblies, and 2D drawings. The following figure shows the design process in SolidWorks.

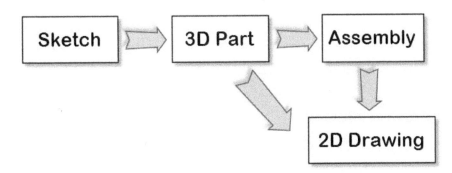

In SolidWorks, you create parts by combining features.

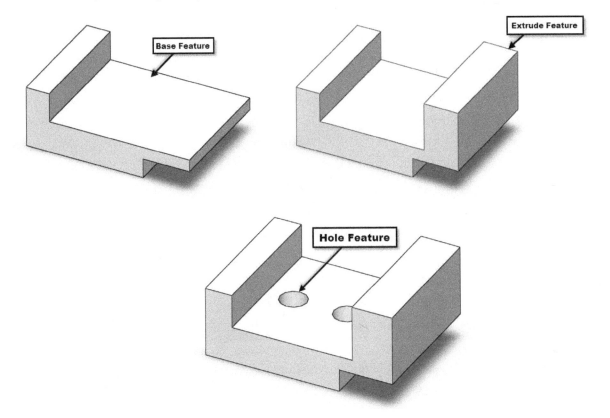

In SolidWorks, features are of two types: sketch-based and placed. You create a sketch based feature by drawing a sketch and extruding, revolving, sweeping along a path, or lofting it.

You create placed features by simply placing them onto an existing feature. Examples of placed features are fillets, chamfers, drafts, shells, holes and so on.

In SolidWorks, parameters, dimensions, or relations control everything. For example, if you want to change the position of the hole shown in figure, you need to change the dimension or relation that controls its position.

Starting SolidWorks

- Click the **Start** button on the Windows taskbar.
- Click **All Programs**.
- Click **SolidWorks 2015 > SolidWorks 2015**.
- Click the **New** button.
- On the **New SolidWorks Document** dialog, click **Part**.
- Click **OK** button

Notice these important features of the SolidWorks window.

User Interface

The following sections explain various components of the user interface.

Menu

Menu is located at top of the window. It has various options (menu titles). When you click on a menu title, a drop-down appears. Select any option from this drop-down.

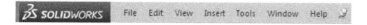

CommandManager

CommandManager is located below the menu. It consists of various tabs. When you click on a tab, a set of tools appear. You can select the required tool from the tab. The following sections explain the CommandManager tabs available in SolidWorks.

Features tab

This CommandManager tab contains the tools to create 3D features.

Evaluate tab

This CommandManager tab has the tools to measure the objects. It also has analysis tools to analyze the draft, curvature, surface and so on.

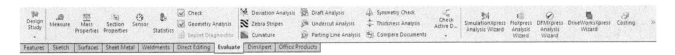

Sketch tab
This tab contains all the sketch tools.

Assemble tab
This CommandManager tab contains the tools to create an assembly. This tab is available in an assembly document.

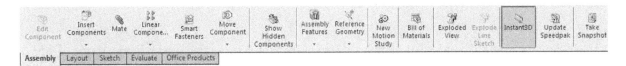

Drawing Environment tabs
In the Drawing Environment, you can create orthographic views of the 3D model. The CommandManager tabs in this environment contain tools to create 2D drawings.

Sheet Metal tab
Use the tools in this tab to create sheet metal components.

Quick Access Toolbar
This is available at the top of the window. It contains the tools such as **New**, **Save**, **Open** and so on.

FeatureManager Design Tree
This is located at the left side of the window. It contains the list of operations carried in a SolidWorks document.

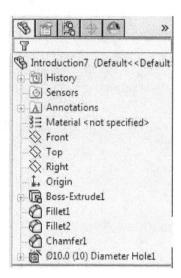

Status bar

This is available below the graphic window. It displays status of the SolidWorks document. For example, if you are drawing a sketch, it displays **Editing sketch**.

View (Heads Up) Toolbar

This is located at the top in the graphics window. It contains the tools to modify the display of the model.

Shortcut Menus

When you click the right mouse button, a shortcut menu appears. A shortcut menu contains a list of some important options.

PropertyManager

When you activate any tool in SolidWorks, the PropertyManager related to it appears. It consists of various options. The following figure shows the components of the PropertyManager.

Mouse Functions

Various functions of the mouse buttons are:

Left Mouse button (MB1)

When you double-click the left mouse button (MB1) on an object, the dimensions related to the object appear. You can then edit the dimensions of the objects.

Middle Mouse button (MB2)

Click and drag this button to rotate the model.

Right Mouse button (MB3)

Click this button to open a shortcut menu.

Mouse Gestures

Customizing the CommandManager, Shortcut Bars, and Menus

To customize the CommandManager, shortcut keys, or menus, click **Options > Customize** on the **Quick Access Toolbar**. On the **Customize** dialog box, use the tabs to customize the CommandManager or menu, or shortcut bars.

Chapter 2: Modeling Basics

This chapter teaches you to construct your first SolidWorks model. You will construct parts of an Oldham Coupling:

In this chapter, you will:
- Construct Sketches
- Construct a base feature
- Add another feature to it
- Construct revolved features
- Construct cylindrical features
- Apply draft

TUTORIAL 1

This tutorial takes you through the creation of your first SolidWorks model. You construct the Disc of the Old ham coupling assembly:

Opening a New Part File

1. To open a new part, click the **New** button on the **Quick Access Toolbar**.

2. On the **New SolidWorks Document** dialog, click **Part**, and then click **OK**.

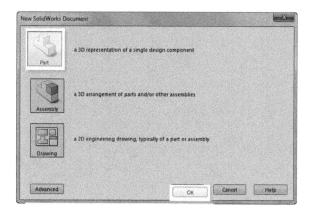

Starting a Sketch

1. To start a new sketch, click **Sketch > Sketch** on the CommandManager.

2. Left click on the front plane.

3. Click **Sketch > Circle** on the CommandManager to start creating a circle.

4. Select the origin point of the coordinate system.
5. Move the pointer away from the origin and click to draw the circle.

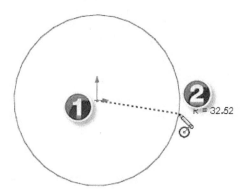

6. Press **ESC** to deactivate the tool.

Adding Dimensions

In this section, you will specify the size of the sketched circle by adding dimensions.

As you add dimensions, the sketch can attain any one of the following three states:

Fully Constrained sketch: In a fully constrained sketch, the positions of all the entities are fully described by dimensions, relations, or both. In a fully constrained sketch, all the entities are black color.

Under Constrained sketch: To define the geometry completely, you need additional dimensions, relations, or both. In this state, you can drag the sketch elements to modify the sketch. An under constrained sketch element is in blue color.

Over Constrained sketch: In this state, an object has conflicting dimensions, relations, or both. An over constraining dimension is in yellow color.

1. Click **Sketch > Smart Dimension** on the CommandManager to start dimensioning the sketch.

2. Select the circle and click; the **Modify** box appears.
3. Type-in **100** in the box and press **Enter** on the keyboard.
4. Press **Esc** to deactivate the **Smart Dimension** tool.
5. To display the entire circle at full size and to center it in the graphics area, use one of the following methods:

• On the **View (Heads Up)** toolbar, click **Zoom to Fit**.

• On the Menu bar, click **View > Modify > Zoom to Fit**.

6. On the CommandManager, click **Sketch > Exit Sketch**.
7. On the **View (Heads Up)** toolbar, click **View Orientation.**
8. Click on the top-right corner of the **View Selector** cube.

Constructing the Base Feature

You can call the first feature of any part as a base feature. You now construct this feature by extruding the sketched circle.

1. On the CommandManager, click **Features > Extruded Boss/Base.**

2. Click on the sketched circle.

3. On the **Boss-Extrude** PropertyManager, type-in **10** in the **Depth** box, and then click **OK**.

Notice the new feature, **Boss-Extrude1**, in the **FeatureManager Design Tree**.

Adding an Extruded Feature

To construct additional features on the part, you must draw sketches on the model faces or planes, and then convert them into features.

1. On the CommandManager, click **Features > Extruded Boss/Base.**
2. Click on the front face of the model.
3. On the CommandManager, click **Sketch > Convert Entities.**

4. Click on the circular edge of the model geometry.

5. On the **Convert Entities** PropertyManager, click **OK**.

6. On the CommandManager, click **Sketch > Line**.

7. Click on the circular edge to specify the first point of the line.

8. Move the pointer towards right.
9. Click on the other side of the circular edge; a line is drawn. In addition, another line is attached to the pointer.

10. Right-click and select **End chain** to end the line.

11. Draw another line below the previous line.

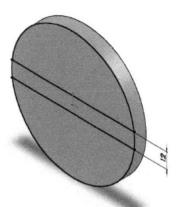

9. Press **Esc** to deactivate the **Line** tool.
10. On the CommandManager, click **Sketch > Display/Delete Relations > Add Relation**.

12. Select the two lines.
13. On the **Add Relations** PropertyManager, under the **Add Relations** section, click **Horizontal** to make the two lines horizontal.
14. Under the **Add Relations** section, click **Equal** to make the lines equal in length.

15. Click **OK** on the PropertyManager.
16. On the CommandManager, click **Sketch > Smart Dimension**.
13. Select the two horizontal lines.
14. Move the pointer toward right and click to locate the dimension.
15. Type-in **12** in the Modify box and click **OK**.

17. On the CommandManager, click **Sketch > Trim Entities**.

18. Click on the arc portions of the projected entity.

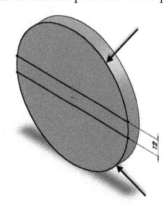

The projected entities are trimmed.

19. Click **OK** on the PropertyManager.

20. On the top right corner of the graphics window, select **Exit Sketch**.

21. On the **Boss-Extrude** PropertyManager, type-in **10** in the **Depth** box, and then click **OK**.

Adding another Extruded Feature

1. Press and hold the Middle Mouse Button and drag the pointer to rotate the part.

2. On the CommandManager, click **Sketch > Sketch**.
3. Click on the back face of the part.
4. Activate the **Convert Entities** tool and convert the circular edge into a sketch entity.

5. Draw two lines, as shown below.

6. Press Esc to deactivate the **Line** tool.
7. Press the Ctrl key and click on the lines.
8. On the PropertyManager, under the **Add Relations** section, click **Vertical**.
9. Click **Equal**, and then click **OK** on the PropertyManager.

10. Activate the **Smart Dimension** tool and apply a dimension of 12 mm distance between the vertical lines.

11. Activate the **Trim Entities** tool and trim the converted entities.

12. Click **Exit Sketch**.
13. Extrude the sketch up to 10 mm depth.

To magnify a model in the graphics area, you can use the zoom tools available on the **View (Heads Up)** toolbar or **View > Modify** menu or on the Shortcut menu.

Click **Zoom to Fit** to display the part full size in the current window.

Click **Zoom to Area**, and then drag the pointer to construct a rectangle; the area in the rectangle zooms to fill the window.

Click **Zoom In/Out**, and then drag the pointer. Dragging up zooms in; dragging down zooms out.

Click on a face, edge, vertex or any object, and then click **Zoom to Selection** on the Context Toolbar. You will zoom to the selection.

To move the part view, click the right mouse button and select **Pan**.

Drag the part to move it around in the graphics area.

Saving the Part

1. Click the **Save** button on the **Quick Access Toolbar**.

2. Enter **Disc** in the **File name** field.
3. Browse to **C:\Users\Username\Documents** folder, and then create a new folder with the name Oldham Coupling.
4. Click **Save** to save the file.
5. Click **File > Close**.

Note:
*.prt or *.sldprt are the file extensions for the files that are created in the Part environment of SolidWorks.

TUTORIAL 2

In this tutorial, you will construct a flange by performing the following operations:

- Constructing revolved feature
- Constructing cut features
- Adding Rounds

Ø30

A

A

50

20

Ø60

12

Ø100

R5

10

SECTION A-A
SCALE 1 : 1

3

6

DETAIL B
SCALE 2 : 1

17

Opening a New Part File

1. To open a new part, click the **New** button on the **Quick Access Toolbar**.
2. On the **New SolidWorks Document** dialog, click **Part**, and then click **OK**.

Sketching a Revolve Profile

Now, you will construct a sketch for the revolved feature.

1. On the CommandManager, click **Sketch > Sketch**.
2. Click on the right plane.
3. Activate the **Line** tool and click somewhere above the vertical axis of the origin.

4. Move the pointer upwards. You will notice that the Vertical relation symbol appears.
5. Click to draw a vertical line.

6. Move the pointer toward left. You will notice that the Horizontal relation symbol appears.
7. Click to draw a horizontal line.

8. Complete the sketch by constructing other lines.

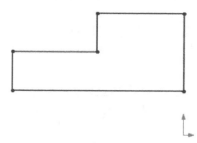

9. On the CommandManager, click **Sketch > Line > Centerline**.

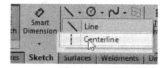

10. Draw a horizontal line passing through the horizontal axis of the coordinate system.

6. Activate the **Smart Dimension** tool and apply to two horizontal dimensions.

7. Click on the centerline and bottom horizontal line.

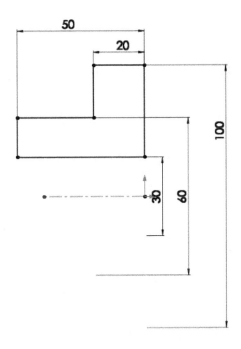

7. Move the pointer downwards right. Click to position the dimension.

10. Click **Exit Sketch**.

Constructing the Revolved Boss

1. On the CommandManager, click **Features > Revolved Boss/Base**.

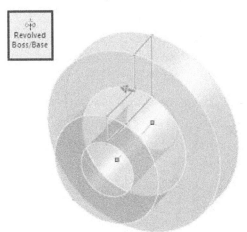

8. Type-in 30 in the **Modify** box and click **OK**.

2. On the **Revolve** PropertyManager, set the **Direction1 Angle** value to **360**.

9. Create other symmetric dimensions, as shown.

3. Click **OK**.

Constructing the Cut feature

1. Press and hold the Middle Mouse Button and drag the pointer to rotate the part.

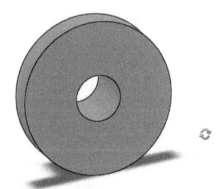

2. Click the right mouse button on the back face and click **Sketch**.

3. On the CommandManager, click **Sketch > Rectangle** drop-down **> Center Rectangle**.

4. Click the origin to define the center point.
11. Move the pointer diagonally toward right and click to create the rectangle.

5. Add dimensions to the sketch.

6. Click **Exit Sketch**.
7. On the CommandManager, click **Features > Extruded Cut**.

8. On the **Cut-Extrude** PropertyManager, set the **Depth** value to 10 and click **OK**.

Constructing another Cut feature

1. Press the right mouse button and drag the mouse to display the Mouse gesture.
2. On the Mouse gesture, select Front.

3. On the CommandManager, click **Sketch > Sketch** and click on the front face.
4. Press **S** on the keyboard.
5. On the Flyout Toolbar, click **Rectangle**.

6. On the PropertyManager, select **Corner Rectangle**.
7. Specify the corners of the rectangle.

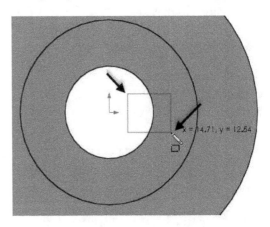

8. On the CommandManager, click **Sketch > Line > Centerline**.
9. Draw a horizontal centerline passing through the origin.
10. Press the Ctrl key and click on the horizontal lines of the sketch.

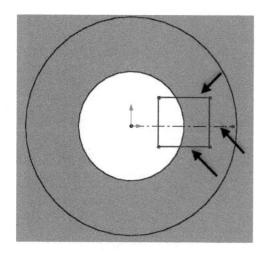

11. On the PropertyManager, under the **Add Relations** section, click **Symmetric**.

12. Click **OK**.
13. Add dimensions to the sketch.

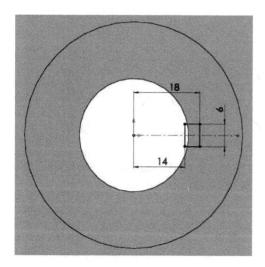

14. Click **Exit Sketch**.
15. On the CommandManager, click **Features > Extruded Cut**.
16. Click on the sketch.

17. On the **Cut-Extrude** PropertyManager, under the **Direction 1** section, select **End Condition > Through All**.

18. Click **OK** to construct the cutout.
19. Press Ctrl+7 on your keyboard to change the view to isometric.

Adding a Fillet

1. Click on the circular edge of the model geometry and select **Fillet**.

2. Enter **5** in the callout attached to the selected edge.

ft="2">ll

Shaded

3. Click **OK** to add the fillet.

Hidden Lines Removed

Hidden Lines Vissible

To display the part in different modes, use the options on the **Display Style** menu on the **View (Heads Up)** toolbar.

Shaded With Edges

Wireframe

The default display mode for parts and assemblies is **Shaded With Edges**. You may change the display mode whenever you want.

23

Saving the Part
1. Click the **Save** button on the **Quick Access Toolbar**.
2. Enter **Flange** in the **File name** field.
3. Browse to **C:\Users\Username\Documents\Oldham Coupling** folder.
4. Click **Save** to save the file.
5. Click **File > Close**.

TUTORIAL 3
In this tutorial, you will construct a Shaft by performing the following operations:

*   Constructing a cylindrical feature
*   Constructing a cut feature

Opening a New Part File
1. To open a new part, click **File > New** on the menu bar.
2. On the **New SolidWorks Document** dialog, click the **Part** button.
3. Click **OK**.

Constructing the Cylindrical Feature
1. Activate the **Revolved Boss/Base** tool and click the right plane.
2. Construct the sketch, as shown in figure.

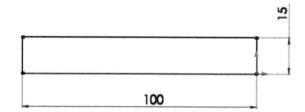

3. Click **Exit Sketch**.
4. Click on the bottom horizontal line of the sketch to define the axis of rotation.

5. Click **OK**.

Constructing Cut feature
1. Activate the **Extruded Cut** tool and click on the front face of the model geometry.
2. On the CommandManager, click **Sketch > Center Rectangle**.
3. Click on the top quadrant point of the circular edge.

4. Move the pointer away and click to construct the rectangle.

5. Add dimensions to the sketch.

6. Click **Exit Sketch**.
7. Click on the extrude handle and drag. A scale appears on the model.
8. Release the pointed when the depth is set to 55.

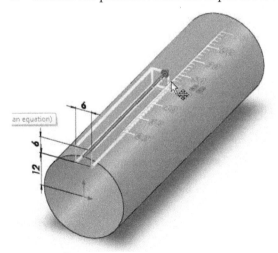

9. Click **OK**.

Saving the Part

1. Click the **Save** button on the **Quick Access Toolbar**.
2. Enter **Shaft** in the **File name** field.
3. Browse to **C:\Users\Username\Documents\Oldham Coupling** folder.
4. Click **Save** to save the file.
5. Click **File > Close**.

TUTORIAL 4

In this tutorial, you construct a Key by performing the following operations:

- Constructing an Extruded Boss
- Applying draft

Constructing Extruded Boss

1. To open a new part, click **File > New** on the menu bar.
2. On the **New SolidWorks Document** dialog, click the **Part** button.
3. Click **OK**.
4. On the CommandManager, click **Features > Extruded Boss/Base**.
5. Click on the front plane.
6. Construct the sketch, as shown in figure.

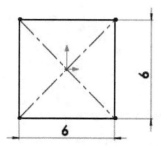

7. Click **Exit Sketch**.
8. On the **Boss-Extrude** PropertyManager, under the **Direction 1** section, set **End Condition** to **Mid Plane**.
9. Set the **Depth** value to 50.
10. Click **OK** to construct the extruded boss.

Applying Draft

1. On the CommandManager, click **Features > Draft**.

2. Click on the front face of the model geometry to define the neutral plane
3. Click on the top face to define the draft face.

4. Type-in 1 in the **Draft Angle** box and click the **Reverse Direction** button.

5. Click **OK**.

Saving the Part

1. Click the **Save** button on the **Quick Access Toolbar**.
2. Enter **Key** in the **File name** field.
3. Browse to **C:\Users\Username\Documents\Oldham Coupling** folder.

4.   Click **Save** to save the file.
5.   Click **File > Close**.

Chapter 3: Assembly Basics

In this chapter, you will:

- Add Components to assembly
- Apply constraints between components
- Create exploded view of the assembly

TUTORIAL 1

This tutorial takes you through the creation of your first assembly. You create the Oldham coupling assembly:

PARTS LIST		
ITEM	PART NUMBER	QTY
1	Disc	1
2	Flange	2
3	Shaft	2
4	Key	2

There are two ways to create any assembly model.

- Top-Down Approach
- Bottom-Up Approach

Top-Down Approach

First, you will start the assembly document, and then construct components in it.

Bottom-Up Approach

First, you will create the components, and then add them to the assembly document. In this tutorial, you will create an assembly using this approach.

Opening a New Assembly File

1. To open a new assembly, click **New** on the **Quick Access Toolbar**.
2. On the **New SolidWorks Document** dialog, click **Assembly**, and then click **OK**.

The Assembly window appears along with the **Begin Assembly** PropertyManager located on the left side.

Inserting the Base Component

1. On the **Begin Assembly** PropertyManager, under the **Part/Assembly to Insert** section, click the **Browse** button.
2. Browse to the location: **C:\Users\Username\Documents\Oldham Coupling**.
3. Double-click on **Flange.** This attaches the component to the pointer.
4. Click inside the graphics window to position the component.

Adding the second component

1. To insert the second component, click **Assembly > Insert Component** on the CommandManager.

2. On the **Insert Component** PropertyManager, click the **Browse** button.
3. Browse to the location **C:\Users\Username\Documents\Oldham Coupling**, and then double-click on **Shaft**.
4. Click inside the graphics window to position the shaft.

Applying Mates

After adding the components to the assembly window, you have to apply mates between them. By applying mates, you establish real contact and motion between components.

You can apply mates between parts using the **Mate** tool.

The following sections explain some of the assembly mates that you can apply using the **Mate** tool.

Coincident: Using this mate, you can align two faces such that they will point in the same direction.

On the context toolbar, click **Flip Mate Alignment** to flip the alignment direction.

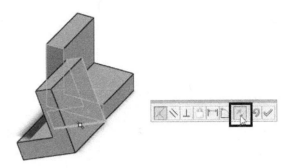

Parallel: Using this mate, you can make an axis, face, or edge of one part parallel to that of another part.

Perpendicular: Using this mate, you can make an axis, face or edge of one part perpendicular to that of another part.

Click **Flip Mate Alignment** to flip the alignment direction. Check the **Lock Rotation** option to lock the rotation between components.

Concentric: Using this mate, you can align the centerlines of the cylindrical faces.

Lock: Makes parts to form a rigid set. As you move a single part in a rigid set, all the other parts will also be moved.

Distance: Applies the distance mate between two components.

Angle: Applies the angle mate between two components.

Click **Flip Dimension** to reverse the angle direction.

Tangent: This mate makes two faces tangent to each other.

1. On the CommandManager, click **Assembly > Mate**.

2. On the **Mate** PropertyManager, click **Concentric**.
3. Click on the cylindrical face of the Shaft.
4. Click on the inner cylindrical face of the Flange

5. Click **Add/Finish Mate**.

This aligns the Shaft and the Flange axially.

6. On the **Mate** PropertyManager, click **Coincident**.
7. Click on the front face of the shaft.

8. Rotate the model.
9. Click on the slot face of the flange, as shown in figure.

10. On the **Mate** PropertyManager, under the **Standard Mates** section, click the **Aligned** button.

11. Click **OK** on the **SolidWorks** message.

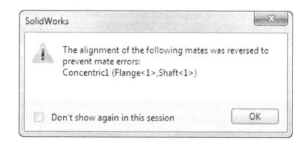

12. Click **Add/Finish Mate**.

This aligns front face of the Shaft and the slot face of the Flange.

Adding the Third Component

1. In order to assemble the third component, you need to hide the Flange. In the **FeatureManager Design Tree**, click the right mouse button on the Flange and select **Hide Components** to hide the Flange. Now, it is easy to assemble the third component.

13. On the **Mate** PropertyManager, click **Coincident**.
14. In the **FeatureManager tree**, expand **Flange** and select **Top Plane**.
15. Expand Shaft and select **Right Plane**.

2. To insert the third component, click **Assembly > Insert Component**.
3. On the PropertyManager, click the **Browse** button.
4. Browse to the folder: **C:\Users\Username\Documents\Oldham Coupling**, and then double-click on the Key.
5. Click inside the graphics window to position the key.

6. Activate the **Mate** tool.
7. On the **Mate** PropertyManager, click **Coincident**.
8. Right-click on the side face of the key and select **Select Other**.

16. Click **Add/Finish Mate**.
17. Click **OK** on the **PropertyManager**.

This assembles the two components and fully constrains the Shaft.

9. From the **Select Other** box, select the bottom face of the Key.

10. Select the bottom face of the slot.

11. Click **Add/Finish Mate**.

This aligns the bottom face of the key with the bottom face of the slot.

12. Select the front face of the Key and back face of the Shaft.

13. Click **Flip Alignment**.

14. Click **Add/Finish Mate**.

This applies the mate between the selected face

15. Click on the top face of the key.

18. Rotate the shaft and select the side face of the slot.

19. Click **Add/Finish Mate**.

20. Click **OK** on the PropertyManager.

Now, you have to turn-on the display of the Flange.

21. Click the right mouse button on the Flange in the **FeatureManager** tree, and then select **Show** to display the Flange.

...

SolidWorks 2015 Learn by doing

Checking the Interference

1. On the CommandManager, click **Evaluate > Interference Detection**.

2. On the PropertyManager, click **Calculate**.

The **Results** section shows **No Interferences.**

3. Click **OK**.

Saving the Assembly

1. Click **Save** on the **Quick Access Toolbar**.
2. Enter **Flange_subassembly** in the **File name** field.
3. Browse to **C:\Users\Username\Documents\Oldham Coupling** folder.
4. Click **Save** to save the file.
5. Click **File > Close**.

Starting the Main assembly

1. Click the **New** button on the **Quick Access Toolbar**.
2. On the **New SolidWorks Document** dialog, click **Assembly**, and then click **OK**.

Adding Disc to the Assembly

1. On the **Begin Assembly** PropertyManager, click **Browse**.

2. Browse to the location **C:\Users\Username\Documents\Oldham Coupling** and double-click on **Disc.ipt**.
3. Click inside the graphics window to place the component at the origin.

Placing the Sub-assembly

1. To insert the sub-assembly, click **Assembly > Insert Components** on the CommandManager.
2. Click **Browse** on the PropertyManager.
3. Browse to the location **C:\Users\Username\Documents\Oldham Coupling** and double-click on **Flange_subassembly.asm**.
4. Click in the window to place the flange sub assembly.

Adding Constraints

1. Activate the **Mate** tool.
2. Click on the front face of the disc and back face of the flange.

36

3. Click **Add/Finish Mate**.
4. Click on top flat face of the disc.

5. Rotate the model geometry and click on the slot face of the flange, as shown in figure.

6. Click **Add/Finish Mate**.
7. Click on the cylindrical faces of the disc and flange.

8. Click **Add/Finish Mate**.
9. Click **OK**.

Placing the second instance of the Sub-assembly

1. Insert another instance of the Flange subassembly.
2. Apply the **Coincident** and **Concentric** relations.

Saving the Assembly

1. Click **Save** on the **Quick Access Toolbar**.
2. Specify **Oldham_coupling** as **File name**.

3. Browse to
   C:\Users\Username\Documents\Oldham Coupling folder.
4. Click **Save** to save the file.

TUTORIAL 2

In this tutorial, you create the exploded view of the assembly:

Creating the Exploded View

1. To create the exploded view, click **Assembly > Exploded View** on the CommandManager.

2. On the **Explode** PropertyManager, under the **Explode Step type** section, click **Regular Step**.
3. On the **Explode** PropertyManager, under the **Options** section, check **Select the subassembly parts**.

4. Click on the shaft, and then click on the Z-axis.

5. On the PropertyManager, under the **Settings** section, set the **Explode Distance** value to **180**.
6. Click **Apply**, and then click **Done**.

7. Click on the flange and set the **Explosion Distance** to 100.
8. Click **Apply**, and then click **Done**.

9. Click on the other shaft and set the **Explosion Distance** to -180.

10. Likewise, explode the other flange to -100 mm distance.

11. Click **OK** on the PropertyManager.

Creating Explode lines

1. To create explode lines; click **Assembly > Explode Line Sketch**.

2. Click on the circular edge of the flange.

3. On the PropertyManager, under the **Options** section, check the **Reverse** option.

4. Click on the circular edge of the shaft.

5. Click **OK**.

6. Click on the vertices of the flange and key, as shown in figure.
7. Click **OK**.

8. Click on the vertices of the flange and disc, as shown in figure.

9. Click **OK**.
10. Click the **Jog Line** button located next to the PropertyManager.

11. Click on the explode line, as shown in figure.

12. Drag the pointer and click to draw a rectangle.

13. Click the **Route Line** icon located next to the PropertyManager.

14. Draw the other explode lines.

15. Click **Exit Sketch**.

The **ConfigurationManager** lists all the explode steps and exploded lines.

To edit an explode step, click the right mouse button on it and select **Edit Feature**.

To collapse the explosion, click the right mouse button on the exploded view and select **Collapse**.

To animate the explosion, click the right mouse button on the exploded view and select **Animate Explode**.

16. Save and close the assembly file.

Chapter 4: Creating Drawings

In this chapter, you create drawings of the parts and assembly from the previous chapters.

In this chapter, you will:

- Create model views
- Create section views
- Create detail views
- Add dimensions and annotations
- Create Custom templates
- Insert exploded view of the assembly
- Insert a bill of materials of the assembly
- Apply balloons to the assembly drawing

TUTORIAL 1

In this tutorial, you will create the drawing of the Flange.sldprt file created in the second chapter.

Opening a New Drawing File

1. To open a new drawing, click the **New** button on the **Quick Access Toolbar**.
2. On the **New SolidWorks Document** dialog, select **Drawing** and click **OK**.

3. On the **Model View** PropertyManager, click **Cancel**.

4. On the **FeatureManager Design Tree**, click the right mouse button on **Sheet1** and select **Properties**.
5. On the **Sheet Properties** dialog, set the **Type of projection** to **Third angle**.
6. Select **A3 (ANSI) Landscape** from the list box in the **Sheet Format/Size** section.

7. Click **OK**.

Generating the Base View

1. On the CommandManager, click **View Layout > Model View**.

2. To generate the base view, click the **Browse** button on the **Model View** PropertyManager.

3. Browse to the location **C:/User/Document/Oldham_Coupling** and double-click on **Flange.sldprt**.
4. On the **Model View** PropertyManager, under the **Orientation** section, click **Front**.

5. Click on the sheet to position the view. The **Projected View** tool gets active.

6. Click **OK** on the **PropertyManager**.
7. On the **View Heads-up** toolbar, click the **Hide > View Origin**. The view origins are hidden.

Creating the Section View

1. To create the section view, click **View Layout > Section View** on the CommandManager.

2. Snap to the center point of the base view and click to position the section line.

3. Click **OK**.

4. Move the pointer toward right and click to place the section view.
5. Click the green check on the PropertyManager.

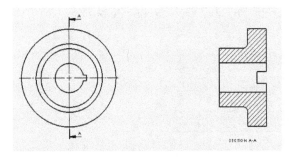

Creating the Detailed View

Now, you need to create the detailed view of the keyway that appears on the front view.

1. To create the detailed view, click **View Layout > Detail View** on the CommandManager.

2. Specify the center point and boundary point of the detail view, as shown in figure.

3. On the PropertyManager, under the **Detail Circle** section, set the options shown below.

4. Set the **Display Style** and **Scale** options, as shown below.

5. Place the detail view below the base view.

Creating the Centerline

1. On the CommandManager, click **Annotation > Centerline**.

2. Click on the inner horizontal edges of the section view, as shown in figure.

3. Click **OK** on the PropertyManager.

Specifying Dimension Settings

1. To specify the dimension settings, click **Options** on the **Quick Access Toolbar**.

2. On the dialog, under the **Document Properties** tab, click **Drafting Standard**.
3. Select **Overall drafting standard > ANSI**.

4. Under **Drafting Standard**, click **Dimensions**.

5. Under **Primary Precision**, select **Unit Precision > None**.

6. At the bottom of the dialog, check the **Center between extension lines**.

7. Click **OK**.

8. At the bottom of the window, set the **Unit System** to **MMGS**.

Retrieving Dimensions
Now, you will retrieve the dimensions that were applied to the model while creating it.

1. To retrieve dimensions, click **Annotation > Model Items** on the CommandManager.

2. On the PropertyManager, select **Source > Entire model**.
3. Uncheck the **Import Items into all views** option.
4. Under the **Dimensions** section, select **Marked for drawing**.

5. Click on the view boundary of the section view and click **OK** on the PropertyManager.

6. Drag and arrange the dimensions.

SECTION A-A

Adding additional dimensions

1. To add dimensions, click **Annotation > Smart Dimension** on the CommandManager.

7. On the section view, click on the fillet edge and position the radial dimension.

SECTION A-A

SECTION A-A

8. Select the radial dimension and click on the arrow to change its direction.

SECTION A-A

9. On the detail view, click on the vertical edge of the slot and position the dimension.

DETAIL B
SCALE 2 : 1

10. Likewise, add dimension to the horizontal edge of the slot.

DETAIL B
SCALE 2 : 1

11. On the CommandManager, click **Annotation > Hole Callout**.

12. Click on the innermost circular edge of the front view and position the hole callout.
13. Click **Close Dialog** on the PropertyManager

Saving the Drawing
1. Click **Save** on the **Quick Access Toolbar**.
2. Specify **Flange** as **Name**.
3. Browse to
   C:\Users\Username\Documents\Oldham Coupling folder.
4. Click **Save** to save the file.
5. Click **File > Close**.

TUTORIAL 2
In this tutorial, you will create the drawing of Disc.sldprt file created in the second chapter.

Creating a Custom Sheet Format
1. On Quick Access Toolbar, click the **New** button.
2. On the **New SolidWorks Document** dialog, select **Drawing** and click **OK**.
3. Close the **Model View** PropertyManager.
4. On the **FeatureManager Design Tree**, click the right mouse button on **Sheet1** and select **Properties**.
5. On the **Sheet Properties** dialog, set the **Type of projection** to **Third angle**.
6. Select **A3 (ANSI) Landscape** from the list box in the **Sheet Format/Size** section.
7. Click **OK**.
8. On the Menu bar, click **Edit > Sheet Format**.

6. Zoom to the title block, and then select the lines and notes shown in figure. Press **Delete** on your keyboard.

7. On the CommandManager, click **Sketch > Line** and draw a line on the title block.

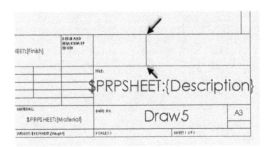

8. On the CommandManager, click **Annotation > Note**.

9. On the PropertyManager, under the **Text Format** section, select **Link to Property**.

10. On the **Link to Property** dialog, select **Current Document**.
11. Select **SW-Author (Author)** and click **OK**.

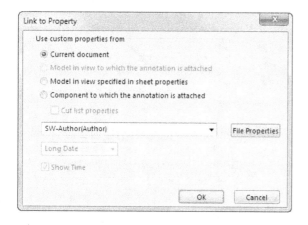

12. On the PropertyManager, under the **Leader** section, select **No Leader**.

13. Click inside the box, as shown in figure.

14. On the **Formatting** toolbar, set the font size to 8 and type **Author**.
15. Click **OK** on the PropertyManager.

16. On the Menu bar, click **Insert > Picture**.
17. Select your company logo and click **Open**.
18. Resize and position the image on the title block.

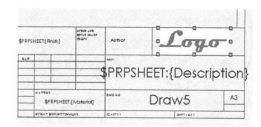

19. Click **OK** on the PropertyManager.
20. Click **Exit Sheet Format**.

21. On the **Quick Access Toolbar**, click **Options**.

22. On the dialog, under the **Document Properties** tab, click **Drafting Standard**.
23. Select **Overall drafting standard >ANSI**.
24. Click **Units** and set the **Unit System** to **MMGS**.
25. Click **OK**.
26. Click **File > Save**.
27. On the **Save As** dialog, select **Save as type > Drawing Templates**.
28. Browse to **C:\Users\Username\Documents\Oldham Coupling** folder.
29. Type-in **Sample** in the **File name** box and click **Save**.
30. On the Menu bar, click **File > Close**.

Starting a New drawing
1. On the Quick Access Toolbar, click the **Options** button.

2. On the **System Options** dialog, click **File Locations**.
3. Select **Show folders for > Document Templates** and click the **Add** button.

4. Browse to **C:\Users\Username\Documents\Oldham Coupling** folder. Click **OK**.
5. Click **OK** on the **System Options** dialog, and then click **Yes**.
6. On the Quick Access Toolbar, click the **New** button.

7. On the **New SOLIDWORKS Document** dialog, click the **Advanced** button.
8. Under the **Oldham Coupling** tab, select **Sample** and click **OK**.

Generating the Drawing Views
1. On the **Model View** PropertyManager, click the **Browse** button and browse to the location: C: /User/Document/Oldham_Coupling
2. Double-click on **Disc.sldprt**.
3. On the PropertyManager, under the **Orientation** section, check the **Create multiple views** option.
4. Select the **Front** and **Bottom** views.

5. Click **OK** on the PropertyManager.

6. On the CommandManager, click **Annotation > Model Items**.
7. On the PropertyManager, select **Source > Entire model**.
8. Click on the two views and click **OK**.

9. Click the right mouse button on the 100-diameter dimension on the front view and select **Display Options > Display as Diameter**.

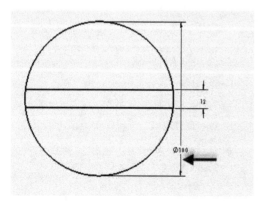

10. Arrange the dimensions by dragging them.

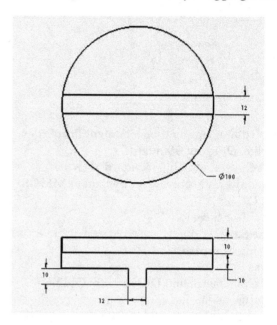

11. Save and close the drawing file.

TUTORIAL 3

In this tutorial, you will create the drawing of Oldham coupling assembly created in the previous chapter.

Creating the Isometric View

1. Start a new drawing file using the **Sample** template.
2. On the **Model View** PropertyManager, click the **Browse** button.
3. Browse to the location C: /User/Document/Oldham_Coupling folder and double-click on **Oldham_Coupling.sldasm**.

4. On the **Model View** PropertyManager, under the **Reference Configuration** section, uncheck the **Show in exploded state** option.
5. Under the **Orientation** section, select **Isometric**.

6. Under the **Scale** section, select **Use custom scale** and set the scale factor to **1:2**.

7. Click on the sheet to position the view.

8. Click the green check on the PropertyManager.

Generating the Exploded View

1. On the CommandManager, click **View Layout > Model View**.
2. On the PropertyManager, under the **Part/Assembly to Insert** section, double-click on **Oldham Coupling**.

3. Under the **Reference Configuration** section, enable **Shown in exploded state**.
4. Under the **Orientation** section, select **Isometric**.
5. Under the **Scale** section, select **Use custom scale** and set the scale factor to **1:2**.
6. Click on the sheet to position the exploded view.

Creating the Bill of Materials

1. Click the right mouse button on the sheet and select **Edit Sheet Format**.
2. Click on the top right corner of the sheet border.

3. Click the right mouse button and select **Set Anchor as > Bill of Materials**.

4. Click **Close Dialog** on the **Point** PropertyManager.
5. Click the right mouse button on the sheet and select **Edit Sheet**.
6. To create a parts list, click **Annotation > Table > Bill of Materials** on the CommandManager.

7. Click on the exploded view.
8. On the PropertyManager, under the **Table Position** section, check the **Attach to anchor point** option.
9. Set the **BOM Type** to **Parts only**.

10. Click **OK**. You will notice that the BOM appears outside the sheet.

11. Click on the anchor point of the BOM.
12. On the PropertyManager, under the **Table Position** section, select **Top Right**.

ITEM NO.	PART NUMBER	DESCRIPTION	QTY.
1	Disc		1
2	Flange		2
3	Shaft		2
4	Key		2

13. Click the green check on the PropertyManager.

Creating Balloons

1. To create balloons, click **Annotation > Auto Balloon** on the CommandManager.

2. On the PropertyManager, under **Balloon Layout** section, select **Layout Balloons to Right**.

3. Click on the exploded view and click **OK**.

4. Save and close the drawing file.

Chapter 5: Sketching

In this chapter, you will learn the sketching tools. You will learn to create:

- Rectangles
- Polygons
- Resolve Sketch
- Relations
- Splines
- Ellipses
- Move, rotate, scale, copy, and stretch entities
- Circles
- Arcs
- Circular pattern
- Trim Entities
- Fillets and Chamfers

TUTORIAL 1 (Creating Rectangles)

A rectangle is a four-sided object. You can create a rectangle by just specifying its two diagonal corners. However, there are various methods to create a rectangle. These methods are explained next.

1. On the CommandManager, click **Sketch > Sketch** and select the Front plane.
2. On the CommandManager, click **Sketch >**

   Rectangle Drop-down > Corner Rectangle

   .

3. Select the origin point to define the first corner.
4. Move the pointer and click to define the second corner.

5. On the PropertyManager, click the **Center Rectangle** icon under the **Rectangle Type** section.
6. Click in the graphics window to define the

center point.
7. Move the pointer and define the corner.

8. On the PropertyManager, select **From Midpoints** under the **Rectangle Type** section.
9. Select the center point and corner point of the rectangle. Two construction lines are created from the midpoints of the rectangles.

10. On the PropertyManager, click the **3 Point Corner Rectangle** icon under the **Rectangle type** section. This option creates a slanted rectangle. You can also check the **Add construction lines** option to add construction lines between the corners or midpoints.
11. Select two points to define the width and inclination angle of the rectangle.

12. Select the third point to define its height.

13. On the PropertyManager, click the **3 Point Center Rectangle** icon under the **Rectangle Type** section.

14. Click to define the center point of the rectangle.
15. Move the pointer and click to define the midpoint of one side.

16. Move the pointer and click to define the corner point.

17. On the PropertyManager, click the

    Parallelogram icon under the **Rectangle Type** section. This option creates a parallelogram by using three points that you specify.
18. Select two points to define the width of the parallelogram.

19. Drag the pointer and click to define the height of parallelogram.

20. Click **Close Dialog** on the PropertyManager.

Lasso Selection
The **Lasso Selection** tool helps you to select multiple elements by dragging the pointer over them.

1. Click the right mouse button and select **Lasso Selection**.

2. Click the left mouse button and drag the pointer covering all the rectangles.

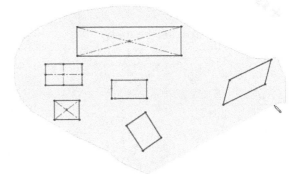

3. Press **Delete** to erase the rectangles.

TUTORIAL 2 (Creating Polygons)
A Polygon is a shape having many sides ranging from 3 to 1024. In SolidWorks, you can create regular polygons having sides with equal length. Follow the steps given next to create a polygon.

1. Activate the **Sketch** mode.
2. On the CommandManager, click **Sketch > Polygon** ⬡.
3. On the PropertyManager, type **8** in the **Number of Sides** box under the **Parameters** section.
4. Select **Inscribed circle**. This option creates a polygon with its sides touching a dotted circle. You can also select the **Circumscribed circle** option to create a polygon with its vertices touching a dotted circle.
5. Click to define the center of the polygon.
6. Move the pointer and click to define the size and angle of the polygon.

7. Press Esc to deactivate the tool.

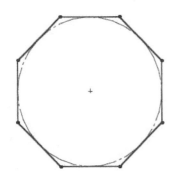

Resolve Sketch

When creating sketches for a part, SolidWorks will not allow you to over-constrain the geometry. The term 'over-constrain' means adding more dimensions than required. The following figure shows a fully constrained sketch. If you add another dimension to this sketch (e.g. diagonal dimension), the **Make Dimension Driven** dialog appears.

Now, you have to convert the new dimension into driven. Select **Make this dimension driven** and click **OK**.

Now, if you change the value of the width, the reference dimension along the diagonal updates, automatically.

TUTORIAL 3 (Relations)

Relations are used to control the shape of a sketch by establishing relationships between the sketch elements. You can add relations using the **Add Relation** tool.

Merge

This relation connects a point to another point.

1. On the **Sketch** tab of the CommandManager, click **Delete/Display Relations > Add Relation**

2. Select two points.
3. Click **Merge** on the PropertyManager. The selected points will be merged.

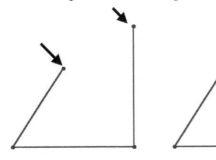

Horizontal

To apply the **Horizontal** relation, click on a line and click the **Horizontal** icon on the context toolbar.

You can also align two points or vertices horizontally. Press the Ctrl key and select the two points. Click the **Horizontal** icon on the PropertyManager.

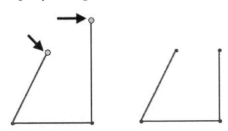

Vertical

Use the **Vertical** relation to make a line vertical. You can also align two vertices vertically by using this relation.

Tangent

This relation makes an arc, circle, or line tangent to another arc or circle. Select a circle, arc, or line. Press the Ctrl key and select another circle, or arc. Click the **Tangent** icon on the PropertyManager. The two elements will be tangent to each other.

Parallel

Use the **Parallel** relation to make two lines parallel to each other.

Perpendicular

Use the **Perpendicular** relation to make two entities perpendicular to each other.

Midpoint

Use the **Midpoint** relation to make a point coincide with the midpoint of a line or arc.

1. Press the Ctrl key and select and line/arc and a point.
2. Click the **Midpoint** icon on the PropertyManager.

TUTORIAL 4 (Midpoint line and Perimeter Circle)

In this tutorial, you will create a sketch using the **Midpoint line** and **Perimeter Circle** tools.

1. Activate the **Sketch** mode.
2. On the CommandManager, click **Sketch > Line drop-down > Midpoint Line** .
3. Click on the origin point to define the midpoint of the line.
4. Move the pointer horizontally and click.

5. Move the pointer upward and click when a dotted line appear from the midpoint of the horizontal line.

6. Create another line closing the sketch.
7. Press Esc to deactivate the **Line** tool.

8. Apply the **Equal** relation between the three the line segments and add a dimension to one segment.

9. On the CommandManager, click **Sketch > Circle drop-down > Perimeter Circle** .
10. Click on the endpoints of three lines. A circle is created passing through the endpoints. Make sure that you click the endpoints when the **Coincident** symbol appears.

11. On the CommandManager, click **Sketch > Display/Delete Relations** .
12. In the PropertyManager, select any tangent relation and click the **Delete** button.

13. Click **OK** on the PropertyManager.
14. Click the right mouse button and select **Recent Commands > Perimeter Circle**.
15. Select the three lines to create a circle tangent to them.

TUTORIAL 5 (Splines)

Splines are non-uniform curves, which are used to create irregular shapes. In AutoCAD, you can create splines by using three methods: **Spline**, **Style Spline**, and **Equation Spline**.

1. Activate the **Sketch** mode.
2. Create a rectangle similar to the one shown below.

3. On the CommandManager, click **Sketch > Spline** .
4. Select the vertices of the rectangle as shown.

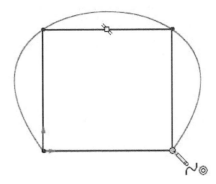

5. Click the right mouse button and select **Select**.
6. On the CommandManager, click **Sketch > Spline drop-down > Style Spline** .
7. Select the vertices of the rectangle, as shown. Notice the difference between the two spline types.

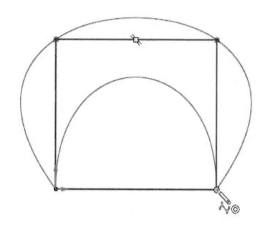

TUTORIAL 6 (Ellipses)

Ellipses are also non-uniform curves, but they have a regular shape. They are actually splines created in regular closed shapes.

1. Activate the **Sketch** mode.
2. On the CommandManager, click **Sketch > Ellipse** drop-down **> Ellipse** .
3. Pick a point in the graphics window to define the center of the ellipse.
4. Move the pointer and click to define the radius and orientation of the first axis.

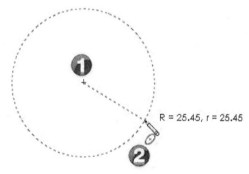

5. Move the pointer and click to define the radius of the second axis.

Partial Ellipse

1. On the CommandManager, click **Sketch > Ellipse drop-down > Partial Ellipse** .
2. Click to define the center of the partial ellipse.
3. Move the pointer and click to define the radius and orientation of the first axis.

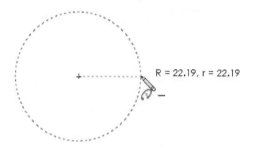

4. Move the pointer and click to define the radius of the second axis and start point.

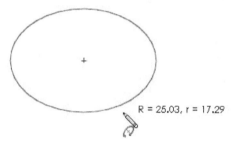

5. Rotate the pointer and click to define end point.

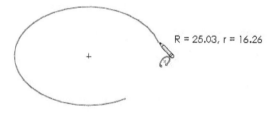

6. Click **Close Dialog** on the PropertyManager.

TUTORIAL 7 (Move and Rotate Entities)

The **Move Entities** tool moves a selected object(s) from one location to a new location without changing its orientation. To move objects, you must activate this tool and select the objects from the graphics window. After selecting objects, you must define the 'base point' and the 'destination point'.

1. Create the sketch as shown below.

2. Click **Sketch > Move Entities** on the CommandManager.

3. Select the square located at the right-side by dragging a selection box, and then right-click to accept the selection.

4. On the PropertyManager, under the **Parameter** section, select **From/To**.

5. Select the lower corner point as the base point.

6. Move the pointer toward right and pick a point as shown below. This moves the square to the new location.

Rotate Entities
The **Rotate Entities** tool rotates an object or a group of objects about a base point.

1. On the CommandManager, click **Sketch > Move Entities > Rotate Entities** .

2. Drag a selection box covering the sketch elements, and click the right mouse button.

3. Click to define the base point of the rotation.

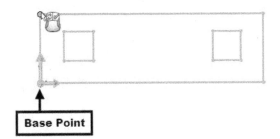

4. Click again and rotate the sketch entities. You can also type-in the rotation angle on the PropertyManager.

5. Click **OK** on the PropertyManager.

TUTORIAL 8
In this tutorial, you will learn to copy, scale, trim entities and perform other operations.

Copy Entities
The **Copy Entities** tool is used to copy objects and place them at a required location. This tool is similar to the **Move Entities** tool, except that object will remain at its original position and a copy of it will be placed at the new location.

1. Draw two circles of 80 mm and 140 mm diameter, respectively.

2. Click **Sketch > Move Entities > Copy Entities** on the CommandManager.

3. Select the two circles, and then right-click to accept the selection.

4. Select the center of the circle as the base point.

5. Move the pointer toward right and click.

This creates a copy of the circles at the new location.

Scale Entities

The **Scale Entities** tool changes the size of objects. It reduces or enlarges the size without changing the shape of an object.

1. Click **Sketch > Move Entities > Scale Entities** on the CommandManager.
2. Select the circles shown below and right-click to accept the selection.

3. Select the center point of the selected circles as the base point.
4. Type 0.6 in the **Scale Factor** box under the **Parameters** section of the PropertyManager.
5. Uncheck the **Copy** option on the PropertyManager and click **OK**.

6. Click **Sketch > Circle drop-down > Perimeter Circle** on the CommandManager.
7. Select the two circles shown below to define the tangent points.

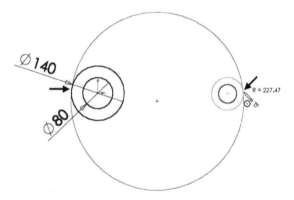

8. Move the pointer down and click to create the circle.

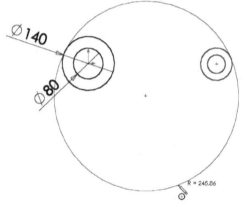

9. Likewise, create another circle by selecting the points as shown.

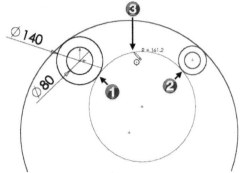

10. Click **Close Dialog** on the PropertyManager.

Trim Entities

When an object intersects with another object, you can remove its unwanted portion by using the **Trim Entities** tool.

1. Click **Sketch > Trim Entities** ⌗ on the CommandManager.

2. On the PropertyManager, click the **Power trim** icon.

3. Press and hold the left mouse button and drag the pointer across the unwanted portions of the circles as shown.

4. On the PropertyManager, click the **Trim Closest** icon.

5. Click on the inner portions of the circles, as shown.

6. Click **Close Dialog** on the PropertyManager.

7. On the CommandManager, click **Sketch > Arc drop-down > 3 Point Arc** .

8. Select three points in the graphics window, as shown.

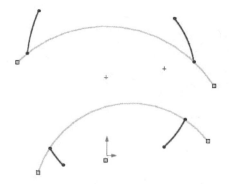

9. Create other arcs using the **3 Point Arc** tool, as shown.

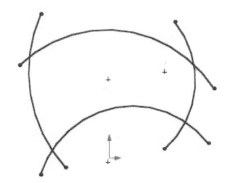

10. On the CommandManager, click **Sketch > Trim Entities**.

11. On the PropertyManager, click the **Trim away inside** icon.

12. Click on the boundary entities, as shown.

13. Click on the entities to trim, as shown.

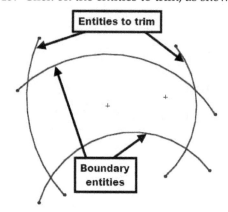

The inner portions of the entities are trimmed.

14. Press Ctrl+Z twice to undo the trim operations (or) click **Undo** twice on the Quick Access Toolbar.

15. Activate the **Trim Entities** tool and click the **Trim away outside** icon on the PropertyManager.

16. Click on the boundary and trim entities. The outer portions are trimmed, as shown.

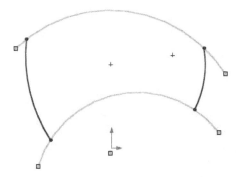

17. Undo the trim operations.

18. Activate the **Trim Entities** tool and click the **Corner** icon on the PropertyManager.

19. Click on the intersecting entities, a shown.

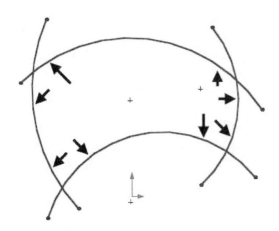

The entities are trimmed to form a corner.

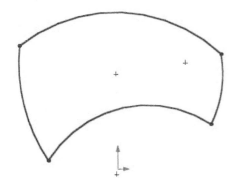

TUTORIAL 9 (Extend Entities)

The **Extend Entities** tool is similar to the **Trim Entities** tool but its use is opposite of it. This tool is used to extend lines, arcs and other open entities to connect to other objects.

1. Create a sketch as shown below.

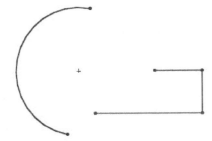

2. Click **Sketch > Trim Entities > Extend Entities** on the CommandManager.

3. Select the horizontal open line. This will extend the line up to arc.

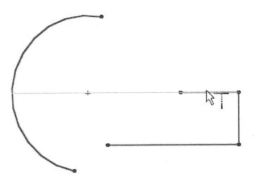

Likewise, extend the other elements, as shown.

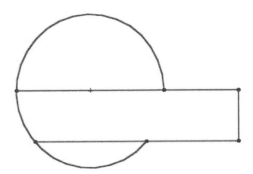

4. Trim the unwanted portions.

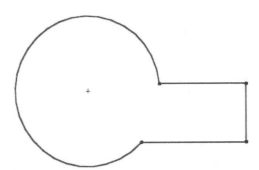

Offset Entities

The **Offset Entities** tool creates parallel copies of lines, circles, arcs and so on.

1. On the CommandManager, click **Sketch** tab > **Offset Entities** .
2. Check the **Select Chain** option on the PropertyManager to select connected elements.
3. Select an entity and notice that all the connected entities are selected.
4. Type-in the offset distance on the PropertyManager.
5. Click inside or outside the sketch to define the offset side.

6. Create a line chain as shown.

7. Activate the **Offset Entities** tool.
8. Select a line segment and notice that entire chain is selected.
9. Check the **Bi-directional** option. Notice that the offset preview appears on both sides.

10. Check the **Cap ends** option and select **Arcs**. Notice that the ends are capped with arcs.

11. Check the **Make base construction** option and click **OK**. The line chain is offset on both sides, and then converted into construction entity.

TUTORIAL 10

This tutorial teaches you to use **Sketch Fillet**, **Sketch Chamfer**, **Mirror Entities**, and **Tangent Arc** tools.

Sketch Fillet

The **Sketch Fillet** tool converts the sharp corners into round corners..

1. Draw the lines as shown below.

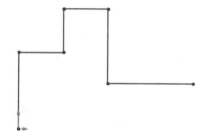

2. Click **Sketch > Sketch Fillet** ⌐ on the CommandManager.
3. On the PropertyManager, type-in a value in the **Radius** box.
4. Click on the corner, as shown.

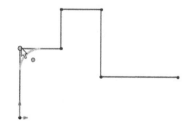

5. Select the vertical and horizontal lines, as shown.

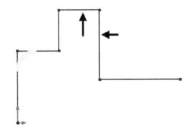

The **Keep constrained corners** option retains all the existing constraints.

The **Dimension each fillet** option dimensions all the fillets created in single instance. If you uncheck this option, only a single fillet is dimensioned and the Equal constraint is applied between all other fillets.

6. Click **OK** on the PropertyManager. The fillets are created. The **Keep visible** icon on the PropertyManager will keep it open. You can select other corners or click the **Close** icon.

Sketch Chamfer

The **Sketch Chamfer** tool replaces the sharp corners with an angled line. This tool is similar to the **Sketch Fillet** tool, except that an angled line is placed at the corners instead of rounds.

1. Click **Sketch > Sketch Fillet > Sketch Chamfer** on the CommandManager.

2. On the PropertyManager, select the **Distance-distance** option and check the **Equal distance** option.

3. Type-in a value in the **Distance** box.

4. Click on the corner as shown.

5. Click **OK** on the PropertyManager.

Mirror Entities

The **Mirror Entities** tool creates a mirror image of objects. You can create symmetrical sketches using this tool.

1. Create a horizontal centerline passing through the origin.

2. On the Command Manager, click **Sketch > Mirror Entities** .

3. Drag a selection box covering all the sketch entities.

4. On the PropertyManager, click in the **Mirror about** box and select the centerline passing through the origin.

5. Click **OK** to mirror the selected entities.

6. On the CommandManager, click **Sketch > Arc drop-down > Tangent Arc** .

7. Select the start point of the arc as shown below.

8. Move the pointer and select the end point of the arc, as shown below.

9. Click **OK** on the PropertyManager.

Stretch Entities

The **Stretch Entities** tool lengthens or shortens drawings or parts of sketches. Note that you cannot stretch circles using this tool. In addition, you must select the portion of the drawing to be stretched by dragging a selection box.

1. On the CommandManager, click **Sketch > Move Entities > Stretch Entities** .

2. Drag a crossing window to select the objects of the sketch, as shown. Click the right mouse button.

1. Create two concentric circles of 140 and 50 diameters.

- Select the base point as shown below.

2. On the CommandManager, click **Sketch > Arc drop-down > Centerpoint Arc** .

3. Select the quadrant point of the circle as shown below.

- Move the pointer toward left and click to stretch the sketch.

4. Move the pointer down and click on the circle when the Coincident symbol appears.

TUTORIAL 11(Circular Sketch Pattern)

The **Circular Sketch Pattern** tool creates an arrangement of objects around a point in circular form.

5. Move the pointer leftwards and up.
6. Click on the circle when the Coincident symbol appears.

7. Click **Close Dialog** on the PropertyManager.
8. Dimension the arc with radius 30.

9. On the CommandManager, click **Sketch > Linear Sketch Pattern > Circular Sketch Pattern** .

10. Select the arc. The preview of the circular pattern appears as the center of the pattern is selected, automatically.

11. Leave the default options on the PropertyManager and click **OK**.
12. Trim the unwanted portions as shown below.

TUTORIAL 12 (3D Sketch)
This tutorial teaches you to create 3D sketches.

1. On the CommandManager, click **Sketch > Sketch drop-down > 3D Sketch**.
2. On the CommandManager, click **Sketch > Line**.
3. Select the origin point to define the start point.

4. Move the pointer along the X-axis and click to create a line.

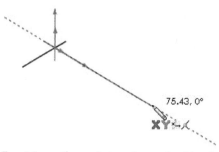

5. Move the pointer along the Y-axis and click.

6. Press the Tab key to change the plane.
7. Move the pointer in the Z-direction and click.

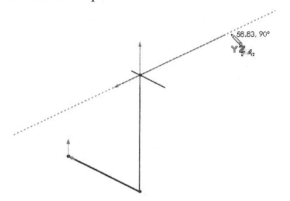

8. Press the Tab key to change the plane.
9. Move the pointer in the X-direction and click.

10. Click the right mouse button and select **Select**.
11. On the CommandManager, click **Sketch > Plane**

12. Press the Ctrl key and select the end points as shown.
13. Click **OK** on the PropertyManager.

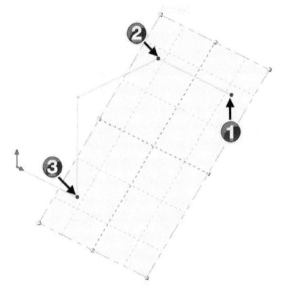

14. Activate the **Line** tool and click the end of the previous line.
15. Move the pointer and click when the **Vertical** symbol appears next to the pointer.

16. Move the pointer and click when the **Horizontal** symbol appears.

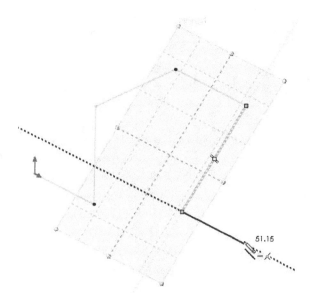

17. Click the right mouse button and select **Select**.
18. Add dimensions and constraints, and then click **Exit Sketch** on the CommandManager.

Chapter 6: Additional Modeling Tools

In this chapter, you construct models using additional modeling tools. You will learn to:

- Construct Helixes
- Add Reference Planes
- Construct Sweep features
- Construct Revolved Cuts
- Mirror Features
- Construct Loft features
- Create multibody parts
- Add Indent Features
- Shell Models
- Create Helical threads
- Construct rib features
- Insert Holes
- Create Patterns

TUTORIAL 1

In this tutorial, you will construct a helical spring using the **Helix** and **Sweep Boss/Base** tools.

Constructing the Helix

1. Open a new SolidWorks file using the **Part** template.
2. To construct a helix, click **Features > Curves > Helix and Spiral** on the CommandManager.

3. Click on the top plane.
4. Draw a circle of diameter 30.

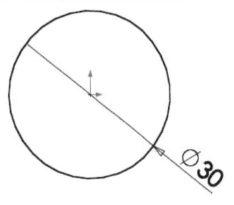

5. Click **Exit Sketch** and change the view to Isometric.

6. On the PropertyManager, set **Pitch** to 10 mm.
7. Set **Revolutions** to 10.
8. Select **Clockwise**.
9. Check the **Taper Helix** option and set **Taper Angle** to 10.
10. Click **OK**.

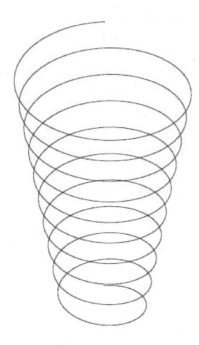

Adding the Reference Plane

1. To add a reference plane, click **Features > Reference Geometry > Plane** on the CommandManager.

2. Select the helix from the graphics window.
3. Select the end of the helix.

4. Leave the default values and click **OK**.

Constructing the Sweep feature

1. On the CommandManager, click **Sketch > Sketch**.
2. Select the plane created normal to helix.
3. On the **View (Heads Up)** Toolbar, click **View Orientation > Normal To**.

4. Draw circle of 4 mm diameter.

5. On the CommandManager, click **Sketch > Display/Delete Relations > Add Relations**.
6. Click on the center point of the circle and helix.
7. On the PropertyManager, under the **Add Relations** section, select **Pierce**.

8. Click **OK**.

9. Click **Exit Sketch** and change the view orientation to Isometric.
10. To construct a sweep feature, click **Features > Sweep Boss/Base** on the CommandManager.

11. Select the circle to define the profile.
12. On the PropertyManager, click in the Path selection box and select the helix to define the path.
13. Leave the default settings and click **OK** to construct the sweep feature.
14. Right-click on the plane and select **Hide** to hide the plane.

15. Save and close the file.

You need to make sure that the size of the cross section is not larger than the curves on the path, the resulting geometry will intersect and the sweep will fail.

TUTORIAL 2

In this tutorial, you construct a pulley wheel using the **Revolve Boss/Base** and **Revolved Cut** tools.

1. Open a file in the **Part** Environment.
2. On the CommandManager, click **Sketch > Sketch**.
3. Click on the right plane.
4. On the CommandManager, click **Sketch > Line > Centerline**.
5. Construct a horizontal centerline passing through origin.
6. Construct the sketch, as shown in figure.

7. Add dimensions to the sketch.
8. Add the **Coincident** relation between the origin and the vertical line at the center.

9. Construct the revolved boss.

Constructing a Revolved Cut

1. To construct a revolved cut, click **Features > Revolved cut** on the CommandManager.

2. Expand the **FeatureManager Design Tree** and select the right plane.
3. Under the **FeatureManager Design Tree**, click the right mouse button on the sketch and select **Normal To**.

4. On the CommandManager, click **Sketch > Convert Entities**.
5. Click on the horizontal edge of the model. Click **OK**.

6. Draw the sketch entities and add dimensions. Trim the unwanted entities.

Constructing a Mirror Feature

1. To construct the mirror feature, click **Features > Mirror** on the CommandManager.

2. Click on the front flat face to define the mirror face.

7. Click **Exit Sketch** and click **OK**.

3. On the PropertyManager, expand the **Bodies to Mirror** section and click on the model geometry.
4. Click **OK**.

5. Save and close the model.

TUTORIAL 3
In this tutorial, you construct a shampoo bottle using the **Loft**, **Extrude**, **Shell**, **Indent**, and **Sweep** tools.

Creating Sections and Guide curves
To construct a lofted boss, you need to create sections and guide curves.

1. Open a new file in the **Part** Environment.
2. On the CommandManager, click **Sketch > Sketch**.
3. Select the top plane.
4. On the CommandManager, click **Sketch > Ellipse**.

5. Select the origin point of the sketch.
6. Move the pointer horizontally and left click.
7. Move the pointer vertically and left click.

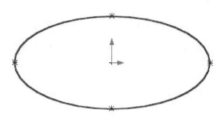

8. Activate **Smart Dimension** tool.
9. Click on the sketch origin and the point on the ellipse, as shown in figure.
10. Type-in **50** in the **Modify** box and click the green check.

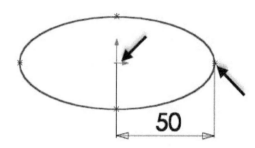

11. Add other dimension to the sketch.

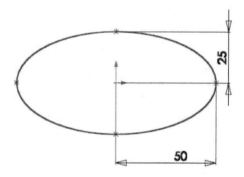

12. On the CommandManager, click **Sketch > Line > Centerline**.
13. Draw a horizontal line passing through the origin and quadrant point.

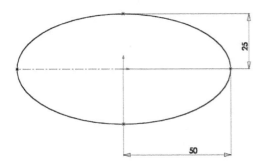

14. Click **Exit Sketch**.
15. Change the orientation to Isometric.
16. On the CommandManager, click **Sketch > Sketch**.
17. Select the front plane.
18. On the CommandManager, click **Sketch > Spline**.

19. Draw a spline similar to the one shown in figure.

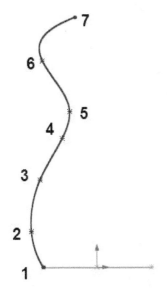

16. Press the Ctrl key and click on the first point of the spline and the previous sketch.
17. On the PropertyManager, under the **Add Relations** section, click **Pierce**.
18. Apply dimensions to the spline, as shown in figure. First, create the horizontal dimensions, and then create the vertical dimensions in descending order.

19. Draw a vertical centerline passing through the sketch origin.
20. On the CommandManager, click **Sketch > Mirror Entities**.

21. Select the spline.
22. On the PropertyManager, click **Mirror about**, and then select the vertical centerline.
23. Click **OK**.

24. Click **Exit Sketch**.
25. Change the view orientation to Isometric.

Creating another section

1. On the CommandManager, click **Features > Reference Geometry > Plane**.

2. Select the top plane from FeatureManager Design Tree.
3. On the PropertyManager, type-in **225** in the **Offset Distance** box.

4. Click **OK**.
5. Start a sketch on the new reference plane.
6. Draw a circle of 40 mm diameter.

7. Click **Exit Sketch**.
8. Change the view to Isometric.

Constructing the swept feature

1. On the CommandManager, click **Features > Lofted Boss/Base**.

2. Select the circle and ellipse.
3. On the PropertyManager, click in the **Guide Curves** selection box and click **OK** on the box.

4. Select the second guide curve and click **OK** on the box.

5. Click **OK**.

the sketch up to 25 mm depth.

Constructing the Extruded feature

1. In the **FeatureManager Design Tree**, expand the Loft feature and select the Sketch 3.

2. Press the Ctrl key and select the reference plane located at the top of the lofted feature.
3. On the Menu bar, click **Insert > Derived Sketch**.

4. Click **Exit Sketch**.
5. Activate the **Extrude Boss/Base** tool and extrude

Adding Fillets

1. On the CommandManager, click **Features > Fillet**.

2. On the PropertyManager, click the **FilletXpert** tab.
3. Click on the bottom and top edges of the loft feature.

4. Set **Radius** to 5 mm.

5. Click **OK** to add the fillet.

Shelling the Model

1. On the CommandManager, click **Features > Shell**.

2. On the PropertyManager, set **Thickness** to 2 mm.
3. Select the top face of the cylindrical feature.

4. Click **OK** to shell the geometry.

Adding the Indent feature

1. On the CommandManager, click **Features > Reference Geometry > Plane**.
2. In the **FeatureManager Design Tree**, select the Front plane.

3. On the PropertyManager, type-in **50** in the **Distance** box.

4. Click **OK**.

5. Create a sketch on the plane, as shown in figure.

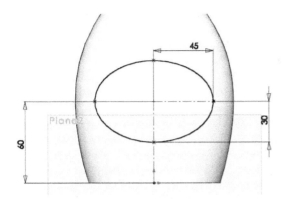

6. Click **Exit Sketch**.
7. On the CommandManager, click **Features > Extruded Boss/Base**.
8. Select the sketch.
9. On the PropertyManager, under the **Direction1** section, select **End Condition > Up To Surface**.
10. On the **PropertyManager**, under **Direction 1**, uncheck **Merge result**.

11. Rotate the model and select the inner face of the model geometry.

12. Click **OK** to create separate extruded body.

13. On the Menu bar, click **Insert > Features > Indent**.

14. Click on the loft feature to define the target body.
15. Click on the extruded body to define the tool body.
16. On the PropertyManager, select **Remove Selections**.
17. Under the **Parameters** section, set the **Thickness** value to 2 and **Clearance** value to 1.

18. Click **OK** to indent the extruded body onto the lofted body.
19. Hide the extruded body, sketch, and plane.

Adding Threads

1. On the CommandManager, click **Features > Reference Geometry > Plane**.
2. Click on the top face of the model geometry.
3. Set the **Distance** value to 5 and check the **Flip offset** option.
4. Click **OK**.

20. Add 1 mm fillet to the inner and outer edges of the indent.

5. Start sketch on the new reference plane.
6. On the CommandManager, click **Sketch > Convert Entities**.
7. Click on the outer edge of the cylindrical feature and click **OK**.

8. Click **Exit Sketch**.

9. On the CommandManager, click **Features > Curves > Helix and Spiral**.
10. Select the circular sketch.
11. On the PropertyManager, select **Constant pitch**.
12. Type-in 7 in the **Pitch** box and check the **Reverse Direction** option.
13. Type-in 2 in the **Revolutions** box.
14. Set the **Start Angle** value to **0**.
15. Uncheck the **Taper Helix** option.
16. Click **OK**.

17. On the CommandManager, click **Features > Reference Geometry > Plane**.
18. Click on the helix and its start point.

19. Click **OK**.
20. Start a sketch on the new reference plane.
21. Draw the thread profile.

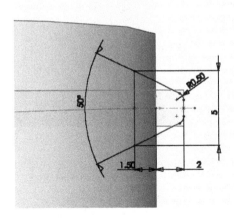

22. Click **Exit Sketch**.

23. On the CommandManager, click **Features > Swept Boss/Base**.
24. Click on the thread profile and the helix.

87

25. On the PropertyManager, expand the **Options** section and check **Merge result**.
26. Click **OK**.

27. Start a sketch on the end face of the thread.

28. On the CommandManager, click **Sketch > Covert Entities** and select the thread profile.

29. Click **OK**.

30. Click **Exit Sketch**.
31. Activate the **Revolved Boss/Base** tool and click on the vertical line of the sketch.
32. On the PropertyManager, set **Direction 1 Angle** to **100**.
33. Check the **Merge result** option.

34. Click **OK**.
35. Rotate the model and click on the other end of the thread.

36. Press the Ctrl key and select the sketch used for the previous revolved feature.
37. On the Menu bar, click **Insert > Derived Sketch**.

38. O n the CommandManager, click
    Display/Delete Relations > Add Relations.
39. Click on the inclined line of the sketch and the
    inclined edge of the end face.

40. On the PropertyManager, click **Collinear**.
41. Click on the end-points, as shown in figure.

42. On the PropertyManager, click **Coincident**.

43. Create a revolved boss using the sketch.

44. Save the model and close it.

TUTORIAL 4

In this tutorial, you construct a patterned cylindrical shell.

Constructing a cylindrical shell

1. Start a new file using the **Part** template.
2. Create a sketch on the top plane.

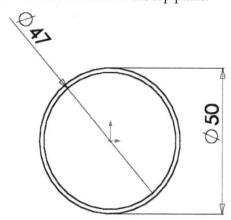

3. Extrude the sketch up to 100 mm depth.

Adding a Slot

1. Activate the **Extruded Cut** tool.
2. Click on the front plane.
3. On the CommandManager, click **Sketch > Straight Slot**.

4. Click to define the first point of the slot.

5. Move the pointer up and click to define the second point.

6. Move the pointer and click to create a slot.
7. Add dimensions to the slot.

8. Click **Exit Sketch**.
9. On the PropertyManager, select **End Condition > Through All**.
10. Click the **Reverse Direction** button next to the **End Condition** drop-down.

11. Click **OK**.

Constructing the Axis

1. On the CommandManager, click **Features > Reference Geometry > Axis**.

2. Click on the inner cylindrical face of the model geometry.

3. Click **OK** to construct the axis.

Constructing the Linear pattern

1. On the CommandManager, click **Features > Linear Pattern**.

2. Select the slot feature.
3. In the FeatureManager Design Tree, select the newly created axis.

4. On the PropertyManager, under the **Direction1** section, set the **Spacing** value to 16.
5. Set **Number of Instances** to 6.

6. Click **OK**.

Constructing the Circular pattern

1. On the CommandManager, click **Features > Linear Pattern > Circular Pattern**.

2. In the FeatureManager Design Tree, select the linear pattern and the cut-extrude feature.

3. On the PropertyManager, click in the **Pattern Axis** selection box and select the cylindrical face of the model.

4. Type-in **12** in the **Number of Instances** box.
5. Type-in **360** in the **Angle** box.
6. Click **OK** to make the circular pattern.

11. Save and close the model.

TUTORIAL 5

In this tutorial, you construct the model shown in figure.

Constructing the first feature

1. Open a new part file.
2. Construct the first feature on the top plane (extrude the sketch up to a distance of 10 mm).

Constructing the Second Feature

1. Draw the sketch on the top face of the first feature.

2. Click **Exit Sketch.**
3. On the CommandManager, click **Features > Extruded Boss/Base.**
4. Type-in **45** in the **Depth** box.

5. Click **OK.**

Constructing the third feature

1. On the CommandManager, click **Features > Reference Geometry > Plane**.
2. Click on the right-side face of the model geometry.

3. Click on the left-side face of the second feature.

4. Click **OK**.

5. Draw the sketch on the new reference plane.

6. Click **Exit Sketch**.
7. On the CommandManager, click **Features > Rib**.

8. On the PropertyManager, click **Thickness > Both Sides**.
9. Set **Rib Thickness** to 10.
10. Select **Extrusion direction > Parallel to Section**.
11. Click **Flip material side**.
12. Click **OK**.

Inserting Holes

1. To insert holes, click **Features > Hole Wizard** on the CommandManager.

2. On the **Hole Specification** PropertyManager, select the **Hole** icon.
3. Select **Standard > ANSI Metric**.
4. Select **Type > Drill Sizes**.
5. Under the **Hole Specifications** section, select **Size > 16**.
6. Select **End Condition > Through All**.
7. Click the **Positions** tab and click on the top face of the base feature.
8. Place two holes on the top face.

9. Add dimensions to define the hole location.

10. Click **OK**.

11. Insert another hole on the front face of the second feature.

Adding Chamfers

1. To add a chamfer, click **Features > Fillet Chamfer** on the CommandManager.

2. On the PropertyManager, select **Distance distance**.
3. Type-in **45** and **25** in the **Distance 1** and **Distance 2** boxes.
4. Click on the corner edge of the first feature.

5. Click **OK** to add the chamfer.

6. Activate the **Chamfer** tool.
7. On the PropertyManager, select **Angle distance**.

8. Type-in **45** in the **Distance** and **Angle** boxes.
9. Click on the corner edge of the second feature.

10. Click **OK**.

TUTORIAL 6

In this tutorial, you create the model shown in figure.

Constructing the first feature

1. Open a new part file.
2. On the CommandManager, click **Features > Extruded Boss/Base**.
3. Click on the top plane.
4. Construct two circles and add dimensions to them.

5. On the CommandManager, click **Sketch > Trim Entities** and trim the intersecting entities.

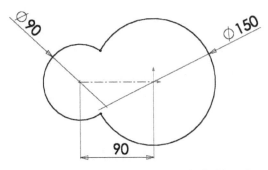

6. On the CommandManager, click **Sketch > Sketch Fillet** and set the **Fillet Radius** value to 10.

7. Select the intersecting corners of the circles, and then click **OK**.

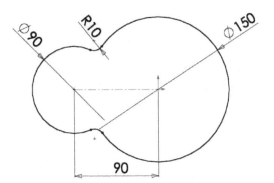

8. Click **Exit Sketch**.
9. Extrude the sketch up to 5 mm depth.

Constructing the Extruded cut

1. On the CommandManager, click **Features > Extruded Cut**.
2. Click on the top face of the model.
3. On the CommandManager, click **Sketch > Convert Entities**.
4. Click on all the edges on the top face.
5. Click **OK**.

6. On the CommandManager, click **Sketch > Offset Entities**.

7. Click on the converted sketch entities.
8. On the PropertyManager, set the **Offset Distance** value to **20**.
9. Check the **Reverse** option.

10. Click **OK**.

11. Click **Exit Sketch**.
12. On the PropertyManager, check the **Flip side to cut** option.
13. Click **OK**.

Constructing the Extruded cut

1. On the CommandManager, click **Features > Extruded Cut**.
2. Click on the top face of the model geometry.
3. On the CommandManager, click **Sketch > Polygon**.

4. On the PropertyManager, type-in 6 in the **Number of Sides** box.
5. Select the **Inscribed circle** option.
6. Click to define the center point of the polygon.

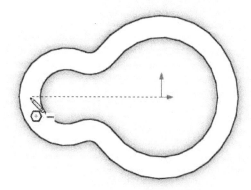

7. Move the pointer and click to construct the

polygon.
8. Draw a horizontal centerline connecting the center point of the polygon and sketch origin.

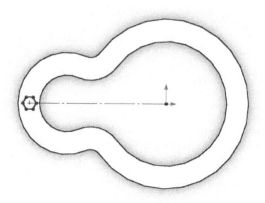

9. On the CommandManager, click **Sketch > Display/Delete Relations > Add Relation**.
10. Click on the horizontal line of the polygon.

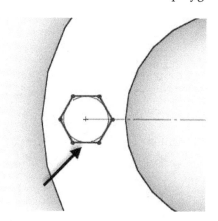

11. On the PropertyManager, click **Horizontal**, and then click **OK**.
12. Add dimensions to the sketch.

13. Click **Exit Sketch**.
14. Create the cut throughout the body.

Making the Curve Driven Pattern

1. On the CommandManager, click **Features > Linear Pattern > Curve Driven Pattern**.

2. In the FeatureManager Design Tree, select the sketch used to create Boss-Extrude1.

3. Select the polygonal cut to define the feature to pattern.

4. Type-in **10** in the **Number of Instances** box.
5. Check the **Equal Spacing** option.

6. Set **Curve method** to **Offset Curve**.
7. Set **Alignment method** to **Tangent to curve**.
8. Click **OK**.

9. Save and close the file.

TUTORIAL 7

In this tutorial, you create a bolt.

Start a new part file

1. Start a new part file using the **Part** template.
2. Construct a cylindrical feature of 20 mm diameter and 75 mm length.

Creating the second feature

1. Start a sketch on the left face of the cylinder.
2. On the CommandManager, click **Sketch > Polygon**.
3. Create a hexagon and dimension it as shown.

4. Exit the sketch.
5. Extrude the sketch up to 12 mm depth.

Adding Cosmetic Threads

1. On the Menu bar, click **Insert > Annotations > Cosmetic Thread**.
2. Click on the right circular edge of the model geometry.
3. Select the right face of the model geometry to define starting point.
4. On the PropertyManager, select **Standard > ANSI Metric** and **Type > Machine Threads**.
5. Select **Size > M20x1.5**.
6. Select **End Condition > Blind** and type-in 40 in the **Distance** box.
7. Click **OK** to add the thread.
8. Save the file as Tutorial7.sldprt.

Creating Configurations Table

Configurations Table allow you to design a part with different variations, sizes, materials and other attributes. Now, you will create different variations of the bolt created in the previous section.

1. Click the **Configurations** tab on the left-side of the window. Notice that there is only one configuration available in the tree.

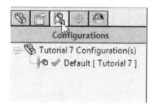

2. Click the **FeatureManager Design Tree** tab.
3. In the FeatureManager Design Tree, expand **Boss-Extrude1** and click the right mouse button on **Sketch1**.
4. Select **Configure Feature** from the shortcut menu.

5. On the **Modify Configurations** dialog, click the down-arrow next to **Sketch1** and check **D1**. Click on the dialog to display the Diameter dimension.

6. On the **Modify Configurations** dialog, click the right mouse button on **Sketch1** and select **Rename**.

7. Type-in **Bolt Diameter** and right-click on the **Modify Configurations** dialog.

8. On the **Modify Configurations** dialog, click in the < *Creates a new configuration.* > cell and type-in Small Diameter. Click on the table to create a new configuration.

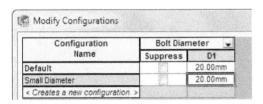

9. Type **12** in the **D1** cell of Small Diameter configuration.

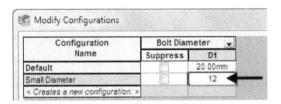

10. In the FeatureManager Design Tree, double-click on **Cosmetic Thread1**, **Boss-Extrude2**, and **Sketch2** to add them to the table.

11. On the **Modify Configurations** dialog, click the right mouse button on **Boss-Extrude2** column and select Delete. The column is removed from the table.

12. Add the dimensions of the **Cosmetic Thread1**and **Sketch2** by click the down-arrows next to columns and checking the dimensions.

13. Modify the D2 value of the Cosmetic Thread1 for Small Diameter configuration to 10.34.

14. Modify the D1 value of the Sketch2 for Small Diameter configuration to 20.

15. On the **Modify Configurations** dialog, type-in **Custom Table** in the box located at the bottom, and then click the **Save table view** button next to it.

16. Click **OK** to close the dialog.

17. Click the **Configurations** tab on the left-side of the window and notice two configurations along with a configurations table.

18. Click the right mouse button on the **Small Diameter** configuration and select **Show Configuration**.

19. To edit the configuration table, click the right mouse button on **Custom Table** and select **Show Table**. The **Modify Configurations** dialog appears. Change the values or create new configurations, and then click the **Save the table view** icon.

20. Save as **Configurations Table.sldprt** and close the file.

TUTORIAL 8

In this tutorial, you create a plastic casing.

Creating the First Feature

1. Open a new Part file.
2. Create a sketch on the Top Plane, as shown in figure.

3. Click **Exit Sketch**.
4. Click the **Features > Extruded Boss/Base** on the CommandManager.
5. Set the **Distance** to 40.
6. Click the **Draft on/off** icon and set the **Draft Angle** to 10.
7. Click **OK**.

Creating the Extruded surface

1. On the CommandManager, click the right mouse on anyone of the tabs and select **Surfaces**.

2. Click **Surfaces > Extruded Surface** on the CommandManager and select the Right Plane.

3. On the View Heads up toolbar, click **View Orientation > Normal To**.

4. Click **Sketch > Spline** on the CommandManager.

5. Create a spline, as shown in figure.

6. Apply dimensions to the spline, as shown below.

7. Click **Exit Sketch**.
8. Set the **End Condition** type to **Mid plane**.
9. Extrude the sketch up to 215 mm depth.

Replacing the top face of the model with the surface

1. On the CommandManager, click **Surfaces >**

Replace Face .

Now, you need to select the face to be replaced.

2. Select the top face of the model.

Next, you need to select the replacement face or surface.

3. Click in the **Replacement Face(s)** box on the PropertyManager and select the extruded surface.
4. Click **OK** to replace the top face with a surface.

5. Hide the extruded surface by clicking on it and selecting **Hide**.

Creating a Face fillet
1. Click the **Fillet** icon on the **Features** panel.
2. Click the **Face Fillet** button on the **Fillet** PropertyManager.
3. Select the top surface as the first face.
4. On the PropertyManager, click in the **Face Set 2** box and select the inclined front face as the second face.

5. On the PropertyManager, under the **Fillet Parameters** section, select **Symmetric** from the drop-down and type 20 in the Radius box. Click **OK** to create the face fillet.

6. Likewise, apply a face fillet of 20 radius between top surface and the back inclined face of the model.

Creating a Variable Radius fillet
1. Click the **Fillet** icon on the **Features** tab.
2. Click the **Variable Size Fillet** icon on the **Fillet** PropertyManager.
3. Click the right mouse button on the curved edge and select **Select Tangency**.

4. Modify the radii values in callouts as shown.

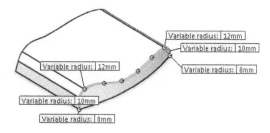

6. Make sure the **Smooth transition** option is checked.
7. Click **OK** to create the variable fillet.

8. Create a variable fillet on other curved edge as shown.

Shelling the Model

1. Click the **Shell** icon on the **Features** tab.

2. On the PropertyManager, type 2.5 mm in the **Thickness** box.

3. Change the orientation of the model and select the bottom face.

4. Click **OK**.

Creating the Mounting Bosses

1. On the CommandManager, click **Features > Axis** .
2. Press the Ctrl key and select the Right and Front planes from the FeatureManager Design Tree.

3. Click **OK** on the PropertyManager.
4. Click **Insert > Fastening Feature > Mounting**

Boss on the Menu bar and select the inside of top surface.

5. Click in the **Select Direction** box on the PropertyManager and select the **Axis** from the FeatureManager Design Tree.
6. Click the **Reverse Direction** icon next to the **Select Direction** box, if the mounted boss appears upwards.
7. Set the **Boss Type** to **Hardware Boss**.
8. Select the **Thread** icon.
9. In the **Boss** section, select **Select mating face**.
10. Select the bottom face of the model geometry.

11. Specify the parameters in the **Boss** section as shown.

12. Specify the parameters in the **Fins** section as shown.

13. In the **Favorite** section, click the **Add or update a favorite** icon.
14. Type **Favorite1** in the **Add or Update a Favorite** dialog and click **OK**.
15. Click **OK** on the PropertyManager to create the boss.

16. In the FeatureManager Design Tree, expand **Mounting Boss1** and notice that a 3D sketch is created.
17. Select **3DSketch1** and click **Edit Sketch**.

18. Press the Ctrl key and select the points as shown.

19. Click the **Coincident** icon on the PropertyManager, and click **OK**.
20. Click **Exit Sketch**. The position of the mounting boss is changed.

21. Likewise, create other mounting bosses as shown.

Creating the Vent Feature

1. Create a sketch on the front inclined face.

2. Click **Exit Sketch**.
3. On the Menu bar, click **Insert > Fastening Feature > Vent** .
4. Select the four lines of the rectangle to define the boundary.

5. Click in the **Ribs** selection box and select the two horizontal lines.

6. Set the rib parameters, as shown below.

7. Click **OK** to create the vent.

8. Save the model as Plastic cover.sldprt and close it.

Chapter 7: Sheet metal Modeling

This chapter will show you to:

- Construct Base Flange
- Construct Edge Flange
- Construct Miter Flange
- Close Corners
- Apply Corner Treatments
- Add Tab features
- Add Jogs
- Unfold and refold the bends
- Cut across bends
- Perform Forming Operations
- Add Hems
- Add Vents
- Add Gussets
- Make Fill Patterns
- View Flat Pattern

TUTORIAL 1

In this tutorial, you construct the sheet metal model shown in figure.

Opening a New File

1. Open a new part file.
2. On the CommandManager, click the right mouse button on anyone of the tabs and select **Sheet Metal**.

The **Sheet Metal** tab appears.

Constructing the Base Flange

1. To construct a base flange, click **Sheet Metal > Base Flange/Tab** on the CommandManager.

2. Select the front plane.
3. Construct the sketch, as shown.

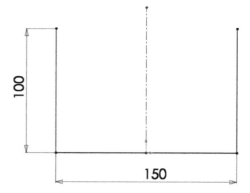

4. Click **Exit Sketch**.
5. On the PropertyManager, under **Direction 1** section, type-in 150 in the **Depth** box.

6. Check the **Use gauge table** option.
7. Select **SAMPLE TABLE –ALUMINIUM-METRIC UNITS**.
8. On the PropertyManager, under the **Sheet Metal Parameters** section, select **Gauge 14.**
9. Set the **Bend Radius** value to **2**.
10. Leave **Auto Relief** to default settings.
11. Click **OK** to construct the base flange.

Adding an Edge flange

1. To add the flange, click **Sheet Metal > Edge Flange** on the CommandManager.

2. Select the edge on the top face.

3. Move the pointer upward and click.
4. On the PropertyManager, under the **Flange Length** section, set **Length** to 100.

5. Click on the **Inner Virtual Sharp** icon in the **Flange Length** section. This measures the flange length from the outer face.
6. Under the **Flange Position** section, click the **Material Outside** icon.
7. Click **OK** to add the flange.

Constructing the Miter Flange

1. To construct the miter flange, click **Sheet Metal > Miter Flange** on the CommandManager.

2. Click the top edge left flange.

3. Draw the sketch, as shown.

4. Click **Exit Sketch**.
5. Click on the vertical edge of the left flange.

3. On the PropertyManager, set the **Corner type** to **Butt**.

4. Rotate the model and select the other corner faces.

6. On the **Miter Flange** PropertyManager, set the

   Flange Position to **Material Inside** and **Gap distance** to 1.25.

7. Under the **Start/End Offset** section, set the **Start Offset Distance** and **End Offset Distance** to **10**.

8. Click **OK** to construct the miter flange.

Closing the Corners

1. To close the corners, click **Sheet Metal > Corners > Closed Corner**.

2. Select the corner face of the miter flange.

5. Click **OK** to close the corners.

Adding Corner Reliefs

1. To add corner reliefs, click **Sheet Metal > Corners > Corner Relief**. This selects the entire part.

2. On the PropertyManager, under the **Corners** section, click **Collect all corners**.

3. Under the **Relief Options** section, set the **Relief** type **Circular** .

4. Type **2** in the **Slot Width** box.

5. Click **OK** to add the corner relief.

The different types of the reliefs are:

Rectangular

Circular

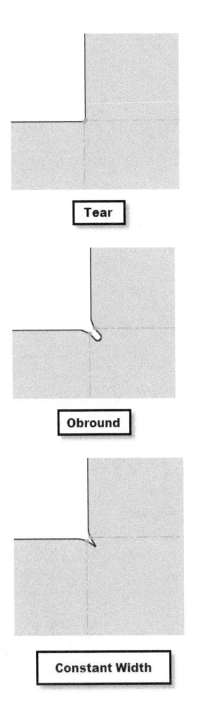

Tear

Obround

Constant Width

Adding a Tab feature

1. To add a tab, click **Sheet Metal > Base Flange/Tab** on the CommandManager.

2. Click on the right side of the base flange.

3. On the CommandManager, click **Sketch > Line**.
4. Click on the vertical edge of the face and move the pointer toward left.
5. Again, click to draw a horizontal line.

6. Move the pointer toward endpoint of the line. The arc mode gets active.

7. Move the pointer toward left, and then downwards.
8. Click to create an arc.

9. Close the sketch and add dimensions.

10. Exit the sketch and click **OK** on the PropertyManager.

Adding a Jog

1. To add a jog, click **Sheet Metal > Jog** on the CommandManager.

2. Click on the tab face and draw a line.

3. Click **Exit Sketch**.
4. Click on the base flange to define the fixed face.

5. On the PropertyManager, under the **Jog Offset** section, set the **Offset Distance** to 20.
6. Set the **Dimension position** to **Outside Offset**
.

7. Set the **Jog Position** to **Bend Centerline** .

8. Set the **Jog Angle** to **75**.
9. Click **OK**.

Unfolding the bends
1. To unfold a bend, click **Sheet Metal > Unfold**.

2. Click on the tab face to define the fixed face.
3. Click on the bends of the jog feature.

4. Click **OK**.

Creating Cuts across bends
1. To create cuts across bends, click **Sheet Metal > Extruded Cut** on the CommandManager.

2. Click on the tab and draw the sketch, as shown.

3. Click **Exit Sketch**.
4. Set the **End Condition** to **Up To Next**.
5. Click **OK** on the PropertyManager.

Folding the Unfolded bends

1. To fold the unfolded bends, click **Sheet Metal > Fold** on the CommandManager.

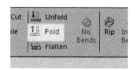

2. Click on the jog bends.

3. Click **OK**.

Performing the Forming Operations

1. To perform forming operations, click **Design Library** on the Task pane.

2. If the Design Library is not displayed, click **Add File Location**.

3. Browse to the location: **C:\ProgramData\SolidWorks\SolidWorks 2015\design library**
4. Click **OK**.
5. In the **Design Library**, click the right mouse button on the **forming tools** folder and select **Forming Tools Folder**.

6. Click **Yes** on the **SolidWorks** message box.

7. Double-click on the **Louvers** folder.

8. Click and drag the Louver onto the flange face.

9. On the PropertyManager, type-in 90 in the **Rotation Angle** box.
10. Under the **Link** section, uncheck the **Link to form tool** option.
11. Under the **Flat Pattern Visibility** section, check the **Override document settings** option.
12. On the PropertyManager, click the **Position** tab and add dimensions to position the louver.

13. Click **OK**.

Making the Linear Pattern

1. On the CommandManager, click **Features > Linear Pattern**.
2. Select the louver feature.
3. Click on the horizontal edge of the flange to define the first direction.
4. On the PropertyManager, under the **Direction 1** section, type-in 50 in the **Spacing** box and 2 in the **Number of Instances** box.
5. Click the **Reverse Direction** button.
6. Click on the vertical edge of the flange feature to define the second direction.
7. Under the **Direction 2** section, type-in **20** in the **Spacing** box and 4 in the **Number of Instances** box.

8. Click **OK** to construct the pattern.

Adding a Hem

1. To add a hem, click **Sheet Metal > Hem** on the CommandManager.

2. Click on the inner edge of the right side flange.

3. On the PropertyManager, under the **Type and Size** section, click the **Closed** icon.
4. Type-in **15** in the **Length** box.

5. Click **OK** to add the hem.

Adding a vent

1. Construct a sketch on the right side face of the base flange.

2. Click **Exit Sketch**.

3. On the CommandManager, click **Sheet Metal > Vent**.

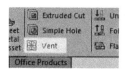

4. Click on the outer most circle of the sketch to define the boundary of the vent.

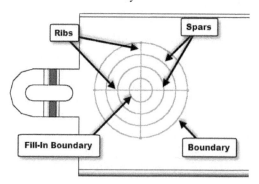

5. On the PropertyManager, click in **Ribs** selection box and select the line segments from the sketch.
6. Type-in 2 in the **Width** box.
7. Click in the **Spars** selection box and select the two middle circles.
8. Type-in 2 in the **Width** box.
9. Click in the **Fill-In Boundary** selection box and select the inner most circle.
10. Click **OK**.

Adding Sheet Metal Gussets

1. To add gussets, click **Sheet Metal > Sheet Metal Gusset** on the CommandManager.

2. Click on the left side bend face of the base flange.
3. On the PropertyManager, under the **Position** section, set the **Offset** value to 30.
4. Under the **Profile** section, set the **Indent depth** to 12.
5. Click the **Rounded gusset** icon.

6. Under the **Dimensions** section, set the **Indent Width** value to 10.
7. Set **Indent Thickness** to **2**.
8. Set **Side face draft** to 2.

9. Set **Inner corner fillet** and **Outer corner fillet** to 1 and 2, respectively.

10. Click **OK**.

11. Make a linear pattern of the gusset.

Making a Fill Pattern

1. Draw a sketch on the top face of the base flange.

2. Click **Exit Sketch**.
3. To make a fill pattern, click **Features > Linear Pattern > Fill Pattern** on the CommandManager.

12. Mirror the gusset and the linear pattern about the right plane.

4. Select the sketch to define the fill boundary.
5. On the PropertyManager, under the **Features to Pattern** section, select **Create seed cut** and select the **Polygon** icon.
6. Set the options in the **Features to Pattern** section, as shown.

7. Under the **Pattern Layout** section, select the **Perforation** button.
8. Type-in 8 in the **Instance Spacing** box.
9. Set **Stagger Angle** to 46.
10. Set **Margins** to 1.

11. Click **OK** to make the fill pattern.

12. Mirror the fill pattern about the right plane.

View the Flat Pattern

1. To view the flat pattern, click **Sheet Metal > Flatten** on the CommandManager.

2. Again, click the **Flatten** button to switch back to the model view.

3. Save the sheet metal part.

Chapter 8: Top-Down Assembly

In this chapter, you will learn to

- Create a top-down assembly
- Insert fasteners using Toolbox
- Create advanced mates

TUTORIAL 1

In this tutorial, you will create the model shown in figure. You use top-down assembly approach to create this model.

Creating a New Assembly File
1. Click the **New** icon on the Quick Access Toolbar, select the **Assembly** icon, and click **OK**.
2. Click **Cancel** on the **Begin Assembly** PropertyManager.

Creating a component in the Assembly
In a top-down assembly approach, you create components of an assembly directly in the assembly by using the **New Part** tool.

1. On the CommandManager, click **Assembly > Insert Components > New Part** .
2. In the FeatureManager Design Tree, click the Front plane. A new part is created and the **Edit Component** mode is activated.

3. Click **Exit Sketch**.
4. Click **Sketch > Sketch** on the CommandManager and select the Top plane

from the FeatureManager Design Tree.
5. Create the sketch as shown below.

2. Click **Exit Sketch**.
3. Click **Features > Extruded Boss/Base** on the CommandManager and extrude the sketch up to 40 mm.

4. Start a sketch on the top face and draw a circle of **50 mm** diameter.

5. Click **Exit Sketch**
6. Extrude the sketch up to 95 mm distance.

7. On the CommandManager, click **Features > Hole Wizard**.

8. On the PropertyManager, click the **Legacy** icon.

9. On the PropertyManager, select **Type > Counterbored**.

10. In the **Section Dimensions** section, modify the dimensions as shown.

Value	Dimension
25	Diameter
100mm	Depth
30	C-Bore Dia...
12	C-Bore Depth

End Condition

Through All

11. Set the **End Condition** to **Through All**.
12. Click the **Positions** tab and click on the top face of the second feature.
13. Select the origin point of the 3D sketch.

14. Click **OK**.

15. Create a through hole of 12 mm diameter on the first feature.

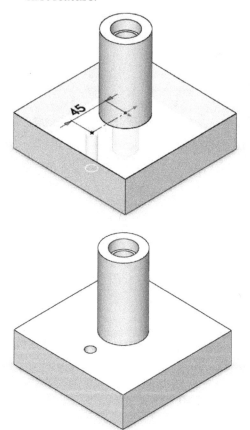

16. Create a circular pattern of the hole.

17. Deactivate the **Edit Component** icon on the CommandManager.

Creating the Second Component of the Assembly

1. On the CommandManager, click **Assembly > Insert Components > New Part** .
2. Select the Front plane of the assembly from the FeatureManager Design Tree.
3. Click **Exit Sketch** on the CommandManager.
4. Click **Sketch > Sketch** on the CommandManager.
5. Select top face of the Base.

6. On the ribbon, click **Sketch > Convert Entities** and select the circular edges of the Base.

7. Draw a circle of 120 mm diameter.

8. Click **Exit Sketch**.
9. Click the outer circle, right-click, click the down-arrows located at the bottom of the shortcut menu, and select **Contour Select Tool**.

10. Click in the region enclosed by the sketch.

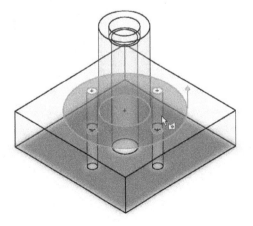

11. Activate the **Extruded Boss/Base** tool and extrude the sketch up to 40.

12. Exit the **Edit Component** Mode.

Creating the third Component of the Assembly

1. On the CommandManager, click **Assembly > Insert Components > New Part** .
2. Select the Front plane of the assembly from the FeatureManager Design Tree.
3. Draw a sketch, as shown in figure.

4. Click **Exit Sketch**.
5. Activate the **Revolve** tool and revolve the sketch.

6. Activate the **Chamfer** tool and chamfer the edges, as shown in figure.

7. Activate the **Fillet** tool and round the edges, as shown in figure.

8. Click **Edit Component** on the CommandManager.

Adding Bolt Connections to the assembly

1. Click the **Design Library** tab on the left side of the graphics window.
2. On the **Design Library** tab, select **Toolbox** and click **Add in now**.
3. On the **Design Library** tab, click **Toolbox >**

ANSI Metric.

4. Under the **ANSI Metric** folder, click **Bolts and Screws > Hex Head**.
5. Click **Heavy Hex Bolt-ANSI B18.2.3.6M** and drag it into the graphics window.

6. On the **Configure Component** PropertyManager, set the bolt properties as shown.

7. Click the **Add** button in the **Part Number** section and click **OK**.
8. Click **OK** on the PropertyManager. Another instance of the bolt is attached to the pointer.

9. Click **Cancel** to stop inserting more bolts.
10. On the **Design Library** tab, click **Washer > Plain Washers**.
11. The **Regular Flat Washer** and drag it into the graphics window.
12. Set the washer size to **M12** and click the **Add** button under the **Part Numbers** section of the PropertyManager.
13. Click **OK** on the **Part Number** dialog.
14. Click **OK** and **Cancel**.

15. On the **Design Library** tab, under **ANSI Metric**, click **Nut > Hex Nuts**.
16. Click and drag **Hex Heavy Nut** into the graphics window.
17. On the **Configure Component** PropertyManager, set the nut properties as shown.

18. Click the **Add** button under the **Part Numbers** section of the PropertyManager.
19. Click **OK** on the **Part Number** dialog.
20. Click **OK** and **Cancel**.

21. On the CommandManager, click **Assembly > Insert Components > New Assembly** . A new sub-assembly is inserted into the assembly.
22. In the FeatureManager Design Tree, click and drag the bolt, nut and washer into the sub-assembly.

23. Click on the assembly and select **Open Assembly**. The Sub-assembly is opened in another window.
24. On the CommandManager, click **Assembly > Mate** .
25. Click the **Multiple mate mode** icon on the PropertyManager.
26. Click the **Concentric** icon on the PropertyManager.
27. Click on the cylindrical face of the bolt, and then click the cylindrical faces of the washer and nut. The bolt face is selected as a common mate entity.

28. Click **Add/Finish Mate** .
29. Select the flat faces of the bolt and washer.

30. Click **Flip Mate Alignment**, and then click **OK** on the **SOLIDWORKS** dialog.
31. Click **Add/Finish Mate**.

32. Likewise, align the end faces of the bolt and nut, and click **OK** on the PropertyManager.

Common Mate Entity

33. Save and close the sub-assembly.
34. On the CommandManager, click **Assembly > Mate**.
35. Click on the flat face for the washer and the part with holes.

36. Click the **Coincident** icon, and click **Add/Finish Mate** .
37. Click the Cylindrical face of the bolt and circular edge of the hole as shown.

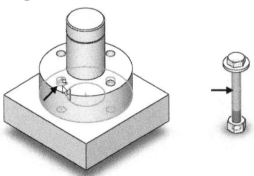

38. Click the **Concentric** icon, check the **Lock Rotation** option, and click **Add/Finish Mate** .
39. Click **OK** on the PropertyManager.

Patterning components in an assembly

1. On the CommandManager, click **Assembly > Linear Pattern > Pattern Driven Component Pattern** .
2. Select the sub-assembly from the FeatureManager Design Tree.
3. On the **Pattern Driven** PropertyManager, click in the **Driving Feature or Component** box.
4. Select the CircularPattern of the first component from the FeatureManager Design Tree.
5. Click **OK** on the PropertyManager.

6. Save the assembly and all its parts.

TUTORIAL 2

In this tutorial, you create a slider crank mechanism by applying advanced mates.

1. Create **Slider Crank Assembly** folder.
2. Download the part files of the assembly from the companion website. Next, save the files in the **Slider Crank Assembly** folder.
3. Start a new assembly file.
4. Click the pin icon on the **Begin Assembly** PropertyManager. This keeps the PropertyManager active.
5. Click the **Browse** button on the PropertyManager.
6. Browse to the **Slider Crank Assembly** folder, select all the components, and click **Open**.
7. On the PropertyManager, in the **Part/Assembly to Insert** section, click **Base**.

8. Click in the assembly window to position the Base component.
9. Likewise, position the other components in the assembly window.
10. Click **OK** on the PropertyManager.

Creating Smart Mates

1. Press the Alt key and click on the face of the slider as shown.

2. Keep the Alt key pressed and drag the component onto the face of the Base as shown.

3. Release the left mouse button and notice that the Mates toolbar appears with the **Coincident** icon selected.
4. Click **Add/Finish Mate** to create the **Coincident** mate between the two faces.
5. Drag the slider up and rotate the view as shown.

6. Click the face of the slider.

7. Press the Alt key and drag the slider onto the face of the Base as shown.

8. Click the **Flip Mate Alignment** icon.
9. Click **Add/Finish Mate**.
10. Click and drag the slider and notice that it can intersect with the base.

Creating the Limit Mate

1. On the CommandManager, click **Assembly > Mate**.
2. On the PropertyManager, expand the **Advanced Mates** section and click the **Distance** ⊢•‖ icon.
3. Select the end face of the Base as shown.

4. Rotate the view and select the end face of the slider as shown.

5. Set the **Distance** value to 1 mm.
6. Set the **Maximum Value** and **Minimum Value** to 459 and 1, respectively.

7. Click **OK** twice on the PropertyManager.
8. Click and drag the slider and notice that it is constrained between the end faces of the slot.

Creating the Slot Mate

1. On the CommandManager, click **Assembly > Mate**.
2. On the PropertyManager, expand the **Mechanical Mates** section and click the **Slot**
    icon.
3. Set the **Constraint** to **Free**.
4. Select the cylindrical face of the pin and flat face of the slider slot as shown.

5. Click **OK** on the PropertyManager.
6. Expand the **Standard Mates** section and click the **Coincident** icon.
7. Select the flat faces of the pin and slider as shown.

8. Click **Add/Finish Mate**, and then click **OK**.
9. Click and drag the pin and notice that it is constrained along the length of the slot.

10. Press the Alt key, click and drag the upper hole of the crank.

11. Release the pointer onto the cylindrical of the pin.

12. Click **Add/Finish Mate** add the **Concentric** mate between the hole and pin.
13. Use the **Mate** command to add the **Coincident** mate between the end face of the pin and flat face of the crank.

14. Assemble the other instance of the pin with the crank.

15. Assemble the pivot with the pin.

16. Make the bottom faces of the pivot and base coincident to each other.

17. Make the Right planes of the pivot and base coincident.

18. Click and drag the crank and notice that the slider moves along the slot.
19. Save and close the assembly and its parts.

Chapter 9: Dimensions and Annotations

In this chapter, you will learn to

- Create Centerlines and Center Marks
- Edit Hatch Pattern
- Apply Dimensions
- Place Hole callouts
- Place Datum Feature
- Place Feature control frame
- Place Surface symbol

TUTORIAL 1

In this tutorial, you create the drawing shown below.

1. Download the Adapter Plate file from the Companion website.
2. Open a new drawing file using the **Sample** template.

3. Click **Cancel** on the **Model View** PropertyManager.
4. In the FeatureManager Design Tree, click the right mouse on Sheet1 and select **Properties**.
5. On the **Sheet Properties** dialog, select **Sheet/Format Size > A4 (ANSI) Landscape**, and then click **OK**.

Creating a Model View with Center Marks

1. On the **Quick Access Toolbar**, click the **Options** icon.
2. Click the **Document Properties** tab on the dialog and select **Detailing** from the tree.
3. Check the options in the **Auto insert on view creation section** as shown.

4. Select **Centerlines/Center Marks** in the tree.
5. Under the **Slot center marks** section, select **Orient to slot** and click the icons as shown.
6. Type-in 1 in the **Size** box.

7. Click **OK**.
8. Click **Layout > Model View** on the CommandManager.
9. Click **Browse** button on the PropertyManager.
10. Browse to the location of the Adapter Plate and double-click on it.
11. Set the **Scale** to **Use sheet scale**.
12. Set the **Orientation** to **Front**.
13. Set the **Display Style** to **Hidden Line Removed**.
14. Place the front view on the left-side on the drawing sheet.
15. Click **OK**.

16. Select the view and press **Delete**.
17. Click **Yes** on the **Confirm Delete** dialog.
18. On the **Quick Access Toolbar**, click the **Options** icon.
19. Click the **Document Properties** tab on the dialog and select **Detailing** from the tree.
20. Uncheck the options in the **Auto insert on view creation section** and click **OK**.
21. Create the front view and notice the difference.

22. Click **Layout > Section View** on the CommandManager.

23. Select the center point of the front view.
24. Click **OK**.
25. Place the section view on the left side.

Creating Centerlines and Center Marks

1. Click **Annotation > Centerline** ⊞ on the CommandManager.
2. Select the parallel lines on the section view, as shown below. The centerline is created.

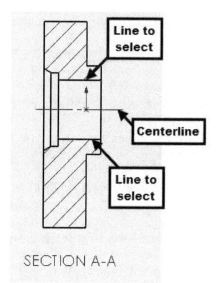

SECTION A-A

3. Click **OK** on the PropertyManager.
4. Click **Annotation > Center Mark** ⊕ on the CommandManager.
5. On the PropertyManager, under **Manual Insert Options** section, click the **Circular Center Mark** ⊕ icon.
6. Select the outer circles of the counterbore holes

7. Click **OK** on the PropertyManager.

8. Activate the **Center Mark** ⊕ command.
9. On the PropertyManager, under the **Auto Insert** section, check **For all slots**.
10. Check the **Circular lines** option and uncheck all other options.
11. Click the **Arc Slot Ends**.
12. Select the front view and click **OK**.

Editing the Hatch Pattern

1. Click on the hatch pattern of the section view. The **Area Hatch/Fill** PropertyManager appears.

SECTION A-A

2. Uncheck the **Material crosshatch** option.

You can select the required hatch pattern from the **Hatch Pattern** drop-down. You can adjust the hatch scale and angle.

3. Click **OK**.

Applying Dimensions

1. Click **Annotation > Model Items** on the CommandManager.
2. Select **Source > Entire model** and uncheck the **Import items into all views** option on the PropertyManager. Click **OK**.
3. Click on the front view.
4. Drag and arrange the dimensions as shown.

5. On the CommandManager, click **Annotation > Hole Callout** ⌴∅.
6. Select the counterbore hole and position the hole callout as shown.

7. On the CommandManager, click **Annotation > Smart Dimension**.
8. Select the center marks of the holes.
9. Move the pointer in the region between the holes and click to position the dimension.

10. Select the R1 dimension and type-in the text in the **Dimension Text** box on the PropertyManager.

11. Click **Close Dialog** on the PropertyManager and position the dimension properly.

12. Dimension the pitch circle diameter of the counterbore holes as shown.

13. On the CommandManager, click **Annotation > Model Items** .
14. Select **Source > Entire model** and uncheck the **Import items into all views** option on the PropertyManager.
15. Click on the section view. Click **OK**.

SECTION A-A

16. Click and drag the dimensions as shown.

17. Select the 2 mm dimension and notice the highlighted origins.
18. Click and drag the endpoints to the new locations as shown.

Destination points

19. Likewise, modify the origins of other dimensions as shown.

20. Select the lines, as shown.
21. Move the pointer toward right and click to place the dimension.

22. Likewise, add the counterbore dimension.

23. Select the counterbore dimension.
24. On the PropertyManager, under the **Tolerance/Precision** section, set the **Tolerance Type** to **Bilateral**.
25. Set the tolerance parameters as shown.

26. Click **Close Dialog**.

SECTION A-A

27. Likewise, apply the other dimensions, as shown below.

Placing the Datum Feature

1. Click **Annotation > Datum Feature** on the CommandManager.
2. Select the extension line of the dimension, as shown below.

3. On the PropertyManager, click the **Filled Triangle with Shoulder** icon.
4. Move the cursor downward and click.
5. Likewise, place a datum feature B, as shown below. Click **OK**.

Placing the Feature Control Frame

1. Click **Annotation > Geometric Tolerance** on the CommandManager.
2. On the dialog, select **Circular Runout** from the **Symbol** drop-down.

3. Type-in **0.02** and **A** in the **Tolerance 1** and **Primary** boxes.
4. Select a point on the line, as shown.
5. Move the cursor horizontally toward right and click.

SECTION A-A

6. On the dialog, select **Circular Runout** from the **Symbol** drop-down.
7. Type-in **0.02** and **B** in the **Tolerance 1** and **Primary** boxes.
8. Select the endpoint of the edge as shown.
9. Move the pointer vertically up and click to position the feature control frame.

10. Likewise, add another feature control frame and click **OK**.

Placing the Surface Texture Symbols

1. Click **Annotation > Surface Symbol** ∇ on the CommandManager.
2. Set the **Maximum Roughness** value to 63 on the PropertyManager.

3. Click on the inner cylindrical face of the hole, as shown below.

4. Click **OK**.
5. Save and close the file.

Additional Exercises

Exercise 1

En tête de page

Exercise 2

Exercise 3

Exercise 4

Exercise 5

Exercise 6

Item Number	File Name (no extension)	Quantity
1	Clamp Jaw	1
2	Spindle	1
3	Spindle Cap	1
4	Handle	1
5	Handle Cap	2

CLAMP JAW

Ø 2 X 45°

22   96   12

Ø 5.5

Ø 20

11   3

M12 x 1.25

Ø 6

SPINDLE

Ø 20

Ø 14   Ø 6.5

2.5

10   Ø 11

SPINDLE CAP

10

M5 ⊽5

1 X 45°

HANDLE CAP

96

5

M5   Ø 5

HANDLE

Chapter 10: Surface Design

SolidWorks Surface modeling tools can be used to create complex geometries that are very difficult to create using solid modeling tools. In addition, you can also use these tools to fix broken imported parts. In this chapter, you will learn the basics of surfacing tools that are mostly used. The surfacing tools are available on the **Surface** Command Manager. You can also find these tools on the menu bar (click **Insert > Surface** on the Menu bar).

If the **Surface** CommandManager is not displayed by default, you can customize it. Right click on any of the tabs of the CommandManager and select **Surface** from the shortcut menu.

SolidWorks offers a robust set of surface design tools. A surface is an infinitely thin piece of geometry. For example, consider a box shown in Figure. It has six faces. Each of these faces is a surface, an infinitely thin piece of geometry that acts as a boundary in 3D space. Surfaces can be simple or complex shapes.

In solid modeling, when you create solid features such as an Extruded Boss or a Revolved Boss, SolidWorks creates a set of surfaces forming a closed volume. This airtight closed volume is considered as a solid body. Although, you can design a geometry using solid modeling tools, the surface modeling tools give you more flexibility.

Creating Basic Surfaces

In this section, you will learn to create basic surfaces using the **Extruded Surface**, **Revolved Surface**, **Swept Surface**, and **Lofted Surface** tools. These tools are similar to that available in solid modeling.

TUTORIAL 1 (Extruded Surfaces)

1. To create an extruded surface, first create an open or closed sketch.

2. Click the **Extruded Surface** button on the **Surface** Command Manager.
3. Select the sketch. The **Surface-Extrude** Property Manager appears and is similar to the **Boss-Extruded** Property Manager.
4. Enter a value in the **Depth** box available in the **Direction 1** section.
5. Click **OK** on Property Manager to create the extruded surface. You will notice that the extrusion was not capped at the ends. You can check the **Cap end** option to cap the ends

TUTORIAL 2 (Revolved Surfaces)

1. To create a revolved surface, first create an open or closed profile and the axis of revolution.

2. Click the **Revolved Surface** button on the **Surface** Command Manager.

3. Select the sketch. The preview of the revolved surface appears.
4. Enter the angle of revolution in the **Direction 1 Angle** box and click **OK**.

Even if you create an enclosed surface, SolidWorks will not recognize it as a solid body. You will notice that the **Mass Properties** button is not available in the **Evaluate** Command Manager. This means that there exists no solid body. You will learn to convert a surface body into a solid later in this chapter.

TUTORIAL 3 (Swept Surfaces)

1. To create a swept surface, create a sweep profile and a path.

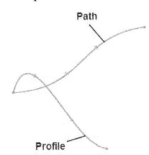

2. Click the **Swept Surface** button on the **Surface** Command Manager (or) click **Insert > Surface > Sweep**.
3. Select the sweep profile and then the path from the graphics window.
4. Click **OK** on the Property Manager.

Various ways of creating swept surfaces are given next.

TUTORIAL 4 (Lofted Surfaces)

1. To create a swept surface, create two or more profiles.

2. Click the **Lofted Surface** button on the **Surface** Command Manager (or) click **Insert > Surface > Loft** on the Menu bar.
3. Select the loft profiles from the graphics window.
4. Click **OK** on the Property Manager.

Various ways of creating lofted surfaces are given next.

Profile 2

Profile 1

Tutorial 5 (Planar Surfaces)

1. To create a planar surface, click the **Planar Surface** button on the **Surface** Command Manager (or) click **Insert > Surface > Planar**.

The PropertyManager prompts you to select the bounding entities. You can select a closed sketch or closed loop of edges.

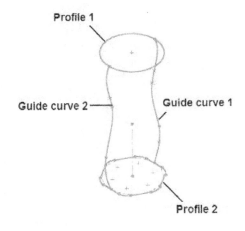

Profile 1

Guide curve 2 —— —— Guide curve 1

Profile 2

Edge to be selected

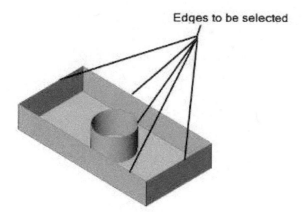

Edges to be selected

2. Select a closed sketch or a closed loop of edges.
3. Click **OK** on the Property Manager. The planar surface will be created.

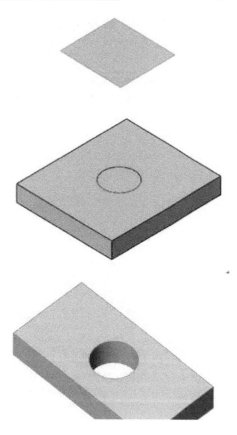

Creating Ruled Surfaces

The **Ruled Surface** tool allows you to create surfaces attached to edges of existing surfaces. You can find the **Ruled Surface** tool on the **Surface** Command Manager. You can also activate this tool from the

menu bar by clicking **Insert > Surface > Ruled Surface**.

You can create five types of ruled surfaces using the options in the Property Manager. These five types of ruled surfaces are discussed next.

TUTORIAL 6 (Creating a Ruled Surface using the Tangent to Surface option)

1. To create a planar surface, click the **Ruled Surface** button on the **Surface** Command Manager (or) click **Insert > Surface > Ruled Surface**.
2. To create this type of ruled surface, select the **Tangent to Surface** option from the **Type** group of the **Ruled Surface** Property Manager.
3. Select an edge from the model.

Edge to be selected

Notice the preview of the ruled surface. The resultant surface will be tangent to the selected edge. In this case, the selected edge is associated with two reference surfaces (the vertical and the top surfaces). As a result, there will be two solutions created from the selected edge. Click the **Alternate Face** button from the **Edge Selection** group to view the alternate solution.

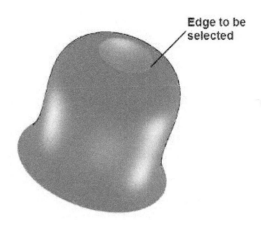

Edge to be selected

4. Enter a distance value in the **Distance** box of the **Distance/Direction** group.

You will notice two options- **Trim and Knit** and **Connecting surface** options available in the **Options** group. These options are useful while creating multiple ruled surfaces at a time. The **Trim and Knit** option, if enabled trims and knits the continuous ruled surfaces. The **Connecting surface** option creates a connecting surface at the sharp corners of the ruled surfaces.

5. Click **OK** to create the ruled surface.

3. Enter a distance value in the **Distance** box of the **Distance/Direction** group.
4. Click the **Reverse Direction** button in the **Distance/Direction** group to reverse the direction, if required.
5. Click **OK** to create the ruled surface normal to the surface on which the selected edge lies.

TUTORIAL 7 (Creating a Ruled Surface using the Normal to Surface option)

1. To create this type of ruled surface, select the **Normal to Surface** option from the **Type** group of the **Ruled Surface** Property Manager.
2. Select an edge from the model.

TUTORIAL 8 (Creating a Ruled Surface using the Tapered to Vector option)

1. To create this type of ruled surface, select the **Tapered to Vector** option from the **Type** group of the **Ruled Surface** Property Manager; some additional options appear in the **Distance/Direction** section.

2. Select a face from the model to define the reference vector.
3. Click on the **Reference Vector** box available in the **Distance/Direction** group.
4. Select an edge from the model.

5. Specify the distance of the ruled surface in the **Distance** box.
6. Specify the taper angle of the ruled surface in **Angle** box available in the **Distance/ Direction** group.
7. Click the **Reverse Direction** button, if required.
8. Click **OK**.

The following figure shows the ruled surface created at a taper angle of 60 degrees.

TUTORIAL 9 (Creating a Ruled Surface using the Perpendicular to Vector option)

1. To create this type of ruled surface, select the **Perpendicular to Vector** option from the **Type** group of the **Ruled Surface** Property Manager.
2. Select a face or an edge to define the reference vector.
3. Select an edge from the model.

4. Specify the distance of the ruled surface in the **Distance** box.
5. Click the **Reverse Direction** button, if required.
6. Click **OK**.

TUTORIAL 10 (Creating a Ruled Surface using the Sweep option)

This option creates a ruled surface by sweeping the selected edge along a reference vector.
1. To create this type of ruled surface, select the **Sweep** option from the **Type** group of the **Ruled Surface** Property Manager.
2. Select a face or an edge to define the reference vector.

You can also use the **Coordinate input** option to define the reference vector.

3. Select an edge or loop of edges from the model.

4. Specify the distance of the ruled surface in the **Distance** edit box.
5. Click the **Reverse Direction** button, if required.
6. Click **OK**.

TUTORIAL 11 (Offset Surface)

1. To create a planar surface, click the **Offset Surface** button on the **Surface** Command Manager (or) click **Insert > Surface > Offset**.
2. Select the faces to offset.

3. Specify the offset distance in the **Offset Distance** edit box.

4. Click **OK** on the Property Manager. The offset surface is created.

TUTORIAL 12 (Knitting Surfaces)

The surfaces created act as individual surfaces unless they are knitted together. The **Knit Surface** tool lets you combine two or more surfaces to form a single surface.

1. To knit surfaces, click the **Knit Surface** button on the **Surface** CommandManager (or) click **Insert > Surface > Knit**.
2. Select the surfaces to knit.

The **Merge entities** option available in the **Selections** section is used to merge the overlapping or redundant surfaces.

The **Try to form solid** option is used to form a solid if the knitted surfaces create a closed volume.

The options in the **Gap Control** group are used to knit the surfaces with small gaps. The **Knitting tolerance** box is used to define a tolerance value for the gaps. The gaps within the specified tolerance value will be knitted. You can also specify the gap range by using the sliders in the **Gap Control** group.

3. After specifying the required options, click the **OK** button to knit the surfaces.

In some cases, you may need to extract the surfaces of the solid body. You can use the **Knit Surface** tool to extract the surfaces of the solid body. Hide the solid body to see the extracted surfaces.

TUTORIAL 13 (Trimming Surfaces)

You can trim surfaces using the **Trim Surface** tool. The surfaces are trimmed using a trimming tool. The trimming tool can be a surface, plane or a sketched entity.

1. To trim a surface, click the **Trim Surface** button on the **Surface** Command Manager (or) click **Insert > Surface > Trim**; the **Trim Surface** Property Manager appears.

You can trim a surface using the **Standard** and **Mutual** options available in the **Trim Type** group. The two trimming methods are discussed next.

Trimming a Surface using the Standard option

2. To trim a surface using this option, click the **Standard** option in the **Trim Types** group.
3. Select **Keep selections** on the PropertyManager.
4. Select the trim tool and surface to keep.

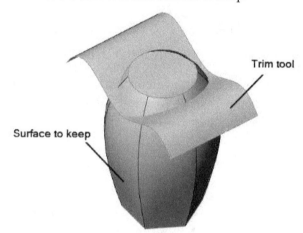

If you select the **Remove selections** option in the **Selections** group, you need to select the surface to remove.

5. Click **OK** to trim the surface.

You can also trim a surface using a sketch.

You can also use a surface as a trim tool that does not extend completely along the surface to be trimmed.

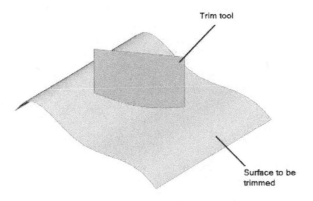

In this case, the **Surface Split Options** will be useful. If you use the **Natural** option, the split will occur following the natural extension of the trim tool.

If you select the **Linear** option, split will be a straight line to the nearest edge.

If you select the **Split All** option, multiple split lines will appear. You can decide which portion of the surface to keep or remove.

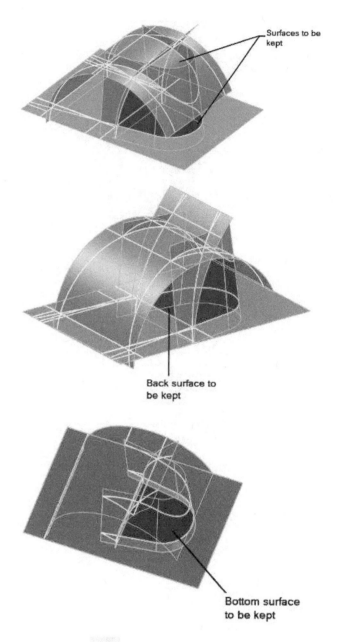

Surfaces to be kept

Back surface to be kept

Bottom surface to be kept

Trimming Surfaces using the Mutual option

The **Mutual** option is used to trim multiple surfaces at a time. For example, you can use this option for the following case.

1. To trim surfaces using this option, select the **Mutual** option from the **Trim Type** group.
2. Select the required surfaces from the model.
3. After selecting the required surfaces, select the **Keep selections** or **Remove selections** option.

If you select the **Keep selections** option, you need to select the surfaces to be kept. If you select the **Remove selections** option, you need to select the surfaces to be removed. In this case, you select the **Keep selection** option.

4. Click in the next selection box of the PropertyManager.
5. Select the surfaces to be kept.

6. Click OK to trim the surfaces.

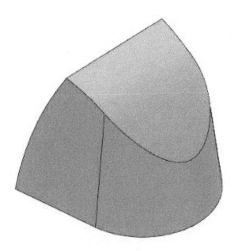

TUTORIAL 14 (Extending Surfaces)

During the design process, you may sometimes need to extend a surface. You can extend a surface using the **Extend Surface** tool.

1. To invoke this tool, click the **Extend Surface** button on the **Surface** Command Manager (or) click **Insert > Surface > Extend**.

The parameters used to define an extended surface are available on this PropertyManager. You can select an edge, multiple edges or an entire surface to extend.

Single edge

Multiple edges

Entire surface

2. Select an edge from the surface body.
3. Select the **Distance** option and type a value in the **Distance** box. If you select the **Up to point** option, you can define the distance by selecting a vertex or point. The **Up to surface** option is used to define the distance by selecting a surface.

When the surface you have selected is not planar, you can decide the type of extension by using the **Extension Type** options. Use the **Same Surface** option to extend the surface by maintaining the curvature of the original surface. If you select the **Linear** option, the extended surface will be created tangent to the original surface.

Linear Extension

4.   Click **OK**.

TUTORIAL 15 (Untrimming a Surface)

You can untrim a trimmed surface using the **Untrim Surface** tool.

1.   Click the **Untrim Surface** button on the **Surface** Command Manager (or) click **Insert > Surface > Untrim**.
2.   Select the edges to be untrimmed.

3.   Click **OK**.

If you select the edge, which is intersecting the boundary of the surface, the untrim surface is created within the boundary. Make sure that the **Edge untrim type** is set to **Extend edges**.

Edge selected

If you check the **Merge to original** option available in the **Options** group, the untrim surface will be merged with the original surface. If you uncheck this option, the untrim surface will be created as an individual surface.

When you untrim the external edges, you have control over the surface created. You can extend the untrim surface beyond the boundary of the surface by entering the extension percentage on the PropertyManager.

Edge selected

If you select the external edges adjacent to each other, the untrim surface will be bound by the selected edges.

Edges selected

If you select the **Connect endpoints** option available in the **Options** group, only the portion necessary to connect the two endpoints is created.

You can use the **Untrim Surface** tool to untrim an entire surface. In addition, the PropertyManager has options to untrim the internal, external, or all the edges of the surface.

Surface selected

TUTORIAL 16(Deleting Holes)

1. To delete a hole, select it from the model and press the **Delete** key. The **Choose Option** dialog appears.

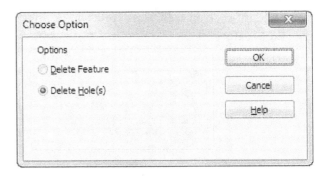

2. Select the **Delete Hole(s)** option and click **OK**.

Hole selected

You will notice the **Delete Hole** feature in the FeatureManager Design Tree.

If you want the hole to be back, you can delete the **Delete Hole** feature from the FeatureManager Design Tree. You can also edit the **Delete Hole** feature. Right-click on the **Delete Hole** feature and click **Edit Feature**.

The **Delete Hole** dialog shows the list of holes that were deleted. You can add more holes to the list by selecting them from the model. You can also remove the hole from the list. Make sure that there is at least one hole in the list.

TUTORIAL 17 (Filled Surface)

The **Filled Surface** tool can be used either to patch holes in models or to create complex surfaces. While patching surfaces, the **Filled Surface** tool gives you more options than deleting holes or untrimming. It provides more control over the definition of the

resultant patch. For example, consider the model shown in figure. You can see that a face is missing. In a case like this, both the **Delete Hole** and **Untrim Surface** tools fail to fill this gap. The **Filled Surface** tool will be used in this case.

1. To create a filled surface, click the **Filled Surface** button on the **Surface** Command Manager (or) click **Insert > Surface > Fill** on the menu bar.

2. To select the patch boundaries, right-click on one of the gap edges and select the **Select Open Loop** option from the shortcut menu. All the gap edges are selected.

3. Select an option from the **Curvature Control** drop-down. This defines the curvature continuity of the fill surface.

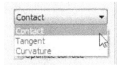

The options in this drop-down are **Contact**, **Tangent**, and **Curvature**. Most of the gap edges should be tangent to the surrounding faces.

The **Apply to all edges** option is used to apply the curvature setting to all edges.

4. Click **OK** to create the filled surface.

TUTORIAL 18

You can also use the **Filled Surface** tool for creating a new surface.

1. Activate the **Filled Surface** tool and select the patch boundary.
2. Click in the **Constraint Curves** selection box and then select the constraint curves.

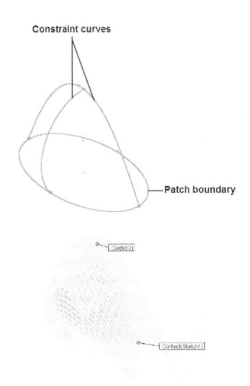

3. Specify the curvature setting (**Contact**, **Tangent**, or **Curvature**).

The **Optimize Surface** option available in the **Patch Boundary** group will create a simple surface very quickly. If you uncheck this option, the **Resolution Control** slider will appear. You can use this slider to define the resulting surface. You can remove wrinkles or other imperfections from the surface. However, the surface will be created very slowly. It is recommended that you use the **Optimize Surface** option for quick results.

4. After specifying the required settings, click **OK** to create the filled surface.

TUTORIAL 19 (Converting a Surface to Solid)

Creating a solid from a surface can be accomplished by simply thickening a surface. You can also create a solid if a volume is enclosed by the surface. For example, consider the surface shown in figure. It encloses a volume. However, there is only one surface body listed in the FeatureManager Design Tree.

1. To make this surface into a solid, click the Thicken button on the **Surfaces** Command Manager.
2. Select the enclosed surface.

You will notice that the **Create solid from the enclosed volume** option is enabled. This option is available only when you select an enclosed surface.

3. Check the **Create solid from the enclosed volume** option.
4. Click **OK** to create a solid.

You can use the **Mass Properties** tool to check whether the surface is converted into a solid or not. You can also use the **Section View** tool.

TUTORIAL 20 (Thickening the Surface)

The **Thicken** tool can also be used to add a thickness to the surface. If the geometry contains more than one surface, than make sure that they are knit together using the **Knit Surface** tool.

1. Activate the **Thicken** command and select the surface to thicken.
2. Type-in the thickness value on the PropertyManager.
3. Define the thickness side using the Thickness buttons. Select the **Thicken Side1** button to add thickness outside the surface. The **Thicken Side2** button is used to add thickness inside the surface. The **Thicken Both Sides** button is used to add thickness to both sides of the surface.
4. Click **OK**.

Thick Both Sides

Thicken Side2

If you have a set of surfaces that enclose a volume, you need to use the **Knit Surface** tool to create a solid.

Tutorial 21 (Deleting Faces)

You can delete unwanted faces from a model. In case of a solid, you can delete a face and make it a surface model.

1. To delete a face, click the **Delete Face** button from the **Surface** Command Manager.
2. Make sure that the **Delete** option is selected in the **Options** group.
3. Select the face to be deleted.

You can also use the **Delete and Patch** option available in the **Options** group. This option will be useful for the following type of cases.

Face to be deleted and patched

1. Select this option from the **Options** group and then select the faces to be deleted.
2. Click **OK**.

The **Delete and Fill** option is used for the following type of cases.

4. Click **OK** to delete the face.

Faces to be deleted

Resulting face is shown next.

TUTORIAL 22 (Replacing Faces)

The **Replace Face** tool replaces a face or group of faces with another face or group of faces.

1. To replace a face, click the **Replace Face** button on the Command Manager (or) click **Insert > Face > Replace** on the Menu bar.
2. Select the target faces for replacement.
3. Click in the **Replacement Surface** selection box and select the replacement surface.

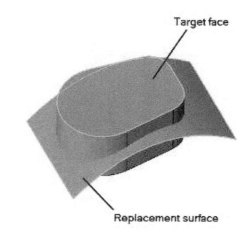

Target face

Replacement surface

4. Click **OK** to replace the surface.

TUTORIAL 23 (Cutting with Surfaces)

You can cut a solid with a surface using the **Cut with Surface** tool. For example, you can cut the solid shown in figure using a surface, and create a complex face on the top.

1. To cut a solid using a surface, click the **Cut with Surface** button on the **Surface** Command Manager (or) click **Insert > Cut > With Surface** from the Menu bar.
2. Select the cutting surface.
3. Specify the direction of the cut using the arrow that appears on the surface.
4. Click **OK**.

The **Bodies to Keep** dialog appears if the cut results in more than one body. Select the **All bodies** option (or) the **Selected Bodies** option and select the bodies to keep from the list. Click **OK** to cut the solid.

TUTORIAL 24 (Thickened Cut)

You can also use the **Thickened Cut** tool to cut a solid with the surface.

1. Click the **Thickened Cut** button on the **Surface** Command Manager (or) click **Insert > Cut > Thicken**.
2. Select the cutting surface.
3. Specify the thickness side.
4. Specify the thickness value.
5. Click **OK**.

TUTORIAL 25 (Freeform Surfaces)

The **Freeform** tool is a powerful tool that is used to create ergonomic shapes. This tool allows you to push and pull a surface to create complex shapes easily. A freeform shape can be created using a face of the solid body or surface.

1. To create a freeform surface, click the **Freeform** button on the **Surface** Command Manager (or) click **Insert > Surface > Freeform** on the Menu bar.
2. Select a face to modify. A mesh appears on the selected surface.

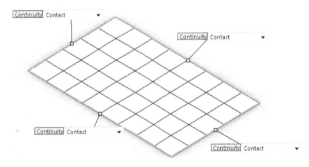

In addition, **Continuity** callouts are attached to the surface boundaries. These callouts are used to control the boundaries of the face. The options in the callouts are **Contact**, **Tangent**, **Curvature**, **Moveable**, and **Moveable/Tangent**.

3. Select **Moveable** from the **Continuity** drop-down. The boundary acts as a control curve.
4. On the PropertyManager, click the **Add Points** button in the **Control Points** group and add control points to the boundary.

5. Click the **Add Points** button again or press ESC.
6. Select a control point on the boundary. A reference triad appears, as shown.

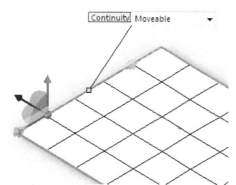

7. Click and drag the Y-axis of the triad and notice the surface. You can use the scale to move the control point precisely.

8. Likewise, drag the Z and X axes to modify the surface.

9. Click and drag the origin of the triad.

Click **Undo** on the PropertyManager, if you want to return to the previous state of the surface. The behavior of the triad can also be controlled using the options in the Property Manager.

You can change the orientation of the triad using the **Global**, **Surface**, and **Curve** options. The **Triad follows selection** option will move the triad along the control point.

10. Select the control curve and notice the tangency control arrows.
11. Drag the tangency control arrows to modify the curvature.

After modifying the surface, if you have by mistake changed the option in the **Continuity** callout, the modifications will be lost.

12. Click the **Add Curves** button in the **Control Curves** group to add control curves on the surface.

You can create two types of control curves- **Through points** and **Control polygon**. The **Through Points** curve is same as discussed earlier in this section. The **Control polygon** is similar to that used while creating a spline.

13. Select the required curve type (**Through points** or **Control polygon**).

14. Move the pointer on the surface. You will notice that a green curve appears on the surface. If you click the **Flip Direction** button in the Property Manager (or) press Tab on your keyboard, the curve will appear in the other direction. You can also switch the direction by pressing the TAB key.

15. Move the pointer and click to specify the location of the control curves. You can create as many curves as possible by clicking at the required locations.

16. Click the **Add Curves** button again or press ESC.

17. Add control points on the control curves by using the **Add Points** button.

18. Select the required control curve; the control points appear on it. Push and pull the control points to modify the surface.

While modifying the surface if you want to change the control curve type (for this example **Though points**), you can select the required option from the **Control Curves** section. The control curve type will be changed.

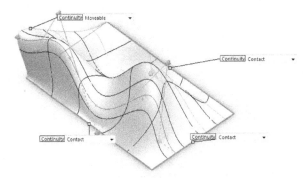

The **Display** section in the Property Manager can be used to modify the display.

19. Drag the **Face transparency** slider to change the transparency of the surface.

20. Drag the **Mesh density** slider to refine the mesh.

21. Display zebra stripes by checking the **Zebra stripes** option.

22. Uncheck the **Zebra stripes** option.
23. Check the **Curvature combs** and **Direction 1** options. The curvature combs appear in the first direction.

You can set the curvature type, scale and density of the curvature combs

24. Click **OK** on the Property Manager.

TUTORIAL 26 (Boundary Surfaces)

The **Boundary Surface** tool is very similar to the **Lofted Surface** tool but allows you to create surfaces that can be tangent, or curvature, continuous in both the directions.

1. To create a boundary surface, click the

Boundary Surface button on the **Surfaces** Command Manager (or) click **Insert > Surface > Boundary Surface** on the Menu bar.

2. Select the curves to define the **Direction 1** of the boundary surface.

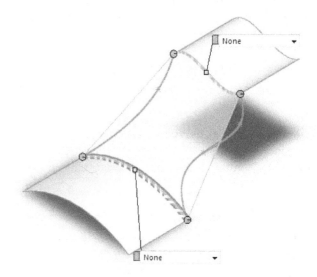

To avoid the twist, make sure that you click on the same side of the two curves. If a twist is created, right-click on anyone of the edges in the **Direction 1** selection box and choose the **Flip Connectors** option.

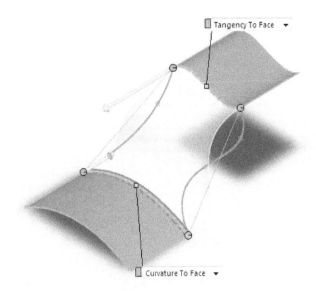

You can specify the way the boundary surface will be connected to the selected edges. To do so, select the required edge from the **Direction 1** selection box. Next, select the **Tangent type** option.

3. Select the **Edge 1** from the **Direction 1** selection box.
4. Select **Tangency To Face** option from the **Tangent type** drop-down (for this example).
5. Specify the tangent length in the **Tangent Length** box or by dragging the arrow displayed on the curve.

8. Click in the **Direction 2** selection box.
9. Select the guide curves.

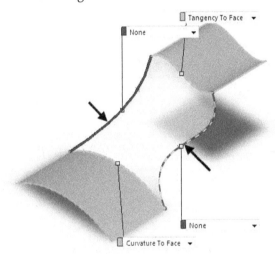

6. Select the **Edge 2** from the **Direction 2** selection box.
7. Select **Curvature To Face** option from the **Tangent type** drop-down (for this example).

You will notice that the **Tangent type** drop-down is replaced by the **Tangent influence** option in the **Direction 1** group. This is just another way to specify the tangent value.

In addition, the **Curve Influence Type** drop-down appears under both the **Direction 1** and **Direction 2** groups. Select the required option from this drop-down.

171

10. Click **OK** to create the boundary surface.

Chapter 11: Mold Tools

In this chapter, you will learn the basics of mold tools in Solidworks. The process of a creating mold is very complex but the in-built mold tools in SolidWorks make it easy for you.

In Solidworks, mold tools are located in the **Mold Tools** CommandManager. You need to customize the Command manager to display this CommandManager. Click the right mouse button on any of the tab in the CommandManager and select **Mold Tools** to display the mold tools.

TUTORIAL 1

In this tutorial, you will design a mold for the part, as shown.

Performing Draft Analysis

1. Download the plastic part from the companion website and open it in SolidWorks.

2. Click the **Draft Analysis** button on the **Mold Tools** CommandManager.

3. Select the Top plane from the FeatureManager Design Tree to specify the Direction of Pull.

4. Set **Draft Angle** to 1 degree.

5. Click **OK**.

The faces displayed in green color are having a positive draft. Whereas, the faces highlighted in red color are having negative draft.

6. Place the pointer on the outer faces of the part and notice the positive draft angle.

7. Place the pointer on the faces highlighted in yellow color. Notice that the draft angle is zero.

You need to apply draft to these faces.

8. Use the **Draft** tool and apply 1 degree draft to all the faces highlighted in yellow.

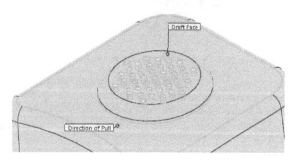

Notice that all the inner faces are red color and outer faces are green.

9. Deactivate the **Draft Analysis** button on the CommandManager.

Applying Shrinkage allowance

Molded parts will shrink after they are removed

from the mold and allowed to cool. To compensate for the shrinkage, you can scale the model to make it slightly larger.

1. To apply a scale feature, click the **Scale** button on the **Mold Tools** CommandManager.

In the **Scale about** drop-down, you can specify the scale factor about the centroid, origin, or coordinate system of the model.

2. For this tutorial, set **Scale about** to **Centroid**.
3. Check **Uniform scaling**.

Note
You can scale the model uniformly or non-uniformly. To scale the model uniformly, check **Uniform scaling**. To scale non-uniformly, uncheck **Uniform scaling** and enter scale factors in the X, Y and Z directions. The non-uniform scaling will result in a deformed shape of the model.

4. Enter 1.02 as **Scale Factor**.
5. Click **OK** to scale the model.

Notice that the scale feature is listed the FeatureManager Design Tree. The scale feature will not affect the size of previously existing features or sketches.

Inserting Mold Folders

SolidWorks adds mold folders to the FeatureManager Design Tree after creating the mold. However, it is recommended that you add the mold folders before creating the mold.

1. On the CommandManager, click **Mold Tools > Insert Mold Folders**.

Creating a Parting Line

A parting line acts as the boundary between the positively and negatively drafted faces of a part. It divides the model into a core and cavity. In addition, the two halves of the mold come into contact at the part line.

1. To create parting line, click the **Parting Lines**
   button on the **Mold Tools** CommandManager.

The parting line uses the draft analysis tool to
determine the positively and negatively drafted
faces. In order to create a parting line, you need to
specify the direction of pull.

2. Select the Top plane from the FeatureManager
   Design Tree to define the direction of pull.

3. Set **Draft Angle** to 1 degree.
4. Make sure that the **Use for Core/Cavity Split**
   and Split faces options are checked.

The **Use for Core/Cavity Split** option is checked to
use the parting line to create the core and cavity.
Note that if there are multiple parting lines created,
the **Use for Core/Cavity Split** option identifies
parting line to be used for splitting the mold.

5. Click the **Draft Analysis** button on the **Parting
   Line** PropertyManager. The parting line appears
   on the model.

The parting line is created at the point where the
positively and negatively drafted faces come
together.

6. Click **OK**   on the PropertyManager. The
   parting line is created and is displayed in the
   FeatureManager Design Tree.

Next, you need to create the shut-off surfaces

Creating Shut-off Surfaces

Shut-off surfaces are necessary when the part being
molded has openings. To create the opening in the
model, the two halves of mold called core and cavity
will have to touch. A shut-off surface is needed to
define the face where the core and cavity will touch.

1. To create shut-off surfaces, click the **Shut-off
   Surfaces**   button on the **Mold Tools**
   CommandManager. The openings on the model
   are detected automatically.

The inner edges of the openings are automatically
selected. These are used to create a shut-off surface.

2. Select **All Tangent**   from the **Reset All Patch
   Types** group.
3. Make sure that the **Knit** option is checked.

Note that the core and cavity surfaces are
automatically created along with the shut-off
surfaces. The core surface acts as the boundary
between the core and the part. The cavity surface
acts as the boundary between the cavity and the
part.

The **Knit** option combines or knits the shut-off
surfaces to the core and cavity surfaces.

4. Rotate the model and notice the redundant loops on the mounting boss holes.

5. Press the Shift key and click on the loops highlighted as redundant. The redundant loops are deselected.
6. Click **OK** to create the shut-off surfaces.
7. To display the results, click the right mouse button on the **Solid Bodies** folder in the FeatureManager Design Tree.

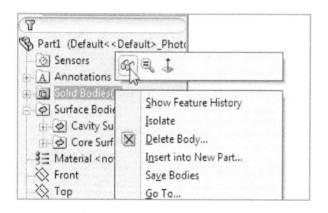

7. Click **Hide** on the Pop-up menu displayed; the core and cavity surfaces are displayed.
8. Expand the **Surface Bodies** folder in the Feature Manager and hide any one of the surfaces to see the other surface.

Core Surface

Cavity Surface

Next, you need to create parting surfaces. In order to do so, you need to hide the core and cavity surfaces and show the solid body.

Creating Parting Surfaces

The parting surfaces extend away from the part and act as contact surface between the core and the cavity blocks.

1. Click on the **Solid Bodies** folder and select **Show**.
2. To create parting surfaces, click the **Parting Surface** button the **Mold Tools** CommandManager.

Now, you need to define the method to create the parting surface.

3. Select the **Perpendicular to pull** option. Notice that the parting line is selected, automatically.

4. Select the **Smooth** icon from the **Parting Surface** group.

5. Type-in 40 in the **Distance** box in the **Parting Surface** section.

6. In the **Options** section, check the **Manual mode** option. Notice the dotted handles on the parting surface.

You can drag these handles to adjust the parting surface.

7. Click **OK** to create the parting surface.

Next, you need to create the mold.

Creating the Tooling Split

First, you need to create a plane that will represent the interface between a core and cavity blocks.

1. Click the **Tooling Split** button on the **Mold Tools** CommandManager and select the parting surface.

2. Create the sketch as shown in figure. You have to make sure that the sketch covers the part completely.

9. Exit the sketch.

10. Specify the **Depth in Direction 1** as 40 in the **Block Size** group.

11. Specify the **Depth in Direction 2** as 10 in the **Block Size** group.

12. Click **OK** to create the mold.

13. Hide the part body, parting surface, core surface, and cavity surface.

10. Click the **Section View** 🔲 icon the View Heads Up toolbar.

11. Click the **Right** ⬜ icon on the PropertyManager.

12. Drag the arrow and notice the gap in the mold. The gap will be filled with material to create the geometry.

13. Click the **Top** ⬜ icon on the PropertyManager and drag the arrow. Notice the gap inside the mold.

14. Click **Cancel** on the PropertyManager.

15. In the FeatureManager Design Tree, expand the **Solid Bodies** folder, click the right mouse button on the tooling split and select **Change Transparency** 🔳 .

16. Likewise, change the transparency of the other tooling split.

17. Click the right mouse button on the part body and select **Show**.

Performing the Undercut analysis

The undercut analysis is performed to detect the portions of the part that cannot be molded using the primary direction of pull.

1. Hide the tooling splits.

2. To perform undercut analysis, click the

   Undercut Analysis button on the **Mold Tools** CommandManager.

Note that the direction of pull is already specified and you do not need to specify it in this case.

Notice the colors displayed on the geometry. Refer to the **Undercut Faces** section on the PropertyManager to get a good understanding of these colors.

The **Direction1 undercut** faces are one, which are not visible from the first pull direction. A single arrow in the graphics window indicates the first pull direction.

The **Direction2 undercut** faces are one, which are not visible from the second pull direction. A double arrow in the graphics window indicates the second pull direction.

Notice the red faces of the model. These are defined as occluded undercuts, which are not visible from either pull directions.

2. Click **OK**   on the PropertyManager.

Direction1 undercut: 49 Faces
Direction2 undercut: 63 Faces
Occluded undercut: 24 Faces
Straddle undercut: 0 Faces
No undercut: 0 Faces

3. Again, click the **Undercut Analysis** button to turn off the colors.

Next, you need to create side cores.

Creating side cores

1. To create a side core, click the **Core** button on the **Mold Tools** CommandManager.
2. Select the inner face of the model, which is having openings.

3. Show the lower tooling split.
4. Create the sketch as shown in figure.

5. Exit the sketch.
6. Click in the **Core/Cavity body** field.

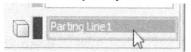

7. Select the upper tooling split from the **Solid Bodies** folder in the **Feature** tree.

8. Click in the **Direction** field.

9. Select the edge of the lower tooling split, as shown.

10. Type-in 4 in the **Draft Angle** box.
11. Select **Through All** from the second drop-down in the **Parameters** group.
12. Uncheck the **Cap ends** option.

13. Click **OK** to create the side core.
14. Hide the other bodies and display the side core body.

14. Likewise, create another side core for the other openings.

15. Show all the solid bodies.
16. On the CommandManager, click **Direct Editing > Move Copy Bodies** .
17. Select the upper tooling split and click the **Translate/Rotate** button on the PropertyManager.
18. Uncheck the **Copy** option.
19. Click and drag the Y-axis of the manipulator.

20. Click **OK**.
21. Likewise, move the bodies as shown.

22. Save the part file.

Creating your own surfaces

1. In the **FeatureManager Design Tree**, click and drag the bar located at the bottom.
2. Release it above the tooling split. The tooling split and cores are suppressed.

3. Show all the surface bodies.
4. Draw a circle on the top face of the cavity surface, as shown.

5. Create an extruded surface with the capped end and draft angle.

6. Hide the Core surface.

7. Trim the Cavity surface, as shown.

8. In the FeatureManager Design Tree, drag the bar and release it below the cores.

9. In the FeatureManager Design Tree, click on the Tooling Split and select the **Edit Feature**.

10. On the PropertyManager, click in the Cavity selection box and select the extruded surface.

11. Click **OK**.
12. Show the cavity solid body and notice the difference.

13. Save and close the file.

Chapter 12: Weldments

SolidWorks provides a set of tools for creating welded frames and structures. In addition to creating welded frames and structures, you can use these tools for different applications. In this chapter, you will learn all of the tools used to create weldments. You will also learn to create custom weldment profiles and add them to your Library.

The weldment tools are located in the **Weldments** Command Manager. You need to customize the CommandManager to display this CommandManager. Click the right mouse button on anyone of the tabs on the CommandManager, and select **Weldments** from the shortcut menu.

TUTORIAL 1

In this tutorial, you create a simple weldment, as shown in figure below.

1. Start a new part file.
2. Click the **Options** button on the Quick access toolbar.
3. Click the **Document Properties** button on the **Options** dialog.
4. Click the **Units** node.
5. Select the **MMGS (millimeter, gram, second)** option.
6. Click the **OK** button to close the dialog.
7. Create a layout sketch on the top plane, as shown.

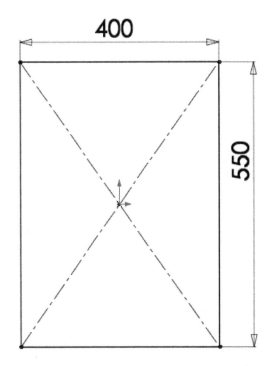

8. Exit the sketch.
9. Click the **Weldments** tab on the Command Manager.
10. Click the **Structural Member** button the **Weldments** tab.

In this **Structural Member** PropertyManager, you need to define the parameters of the structural member.

11. Select **iso** from the **Standard** drop-down.
12. Select **sb beam** from the **Type** drop-down.
13. Select **80X60** from the **Size** drop-down. Next, you need to define the position of the structural members.
14. Select the left vertical line and bottom horizontal line of the layout sketch. A structural member is created on the selected sketch segment.

You will notice that **Group1** is listed in the **Groups** selection box. In addition, the selected segments are listed in the **Path segments** selection box of the **Settings** section.

If you click the **New Group** button, a new group will be created. If you select the line segments from the layout sketch, they will be listed under the second group. Note that the size and parameter settings will be applied to all the groups. If you change the size of the structural member, it will be applied to members of all the groups.

15. Select the other two segments of the layout sketch.

You can control the end condition of the structural members by using the **Apply corner treatment** option in the **Settings** section. By default, this option is checked. As result, the corner treatment is applied between the structural members. If you uncheck this option, the corner treatment will not be applied.

You can change the type of corner treatment by using the icons available below the **Apply corner treatment** option.

By using these icons, the corner treatment can be applied to all the structural members. If you select the **End miter** button, the **Merge miter trimmed bodies** option will be available. This option is used to merge the trimmed bodies into a single body.

If you select the **End butt1** or **End butt2** button, the **Simple cut** and **Coped cut** buttons will be available. The **Simple cut** button is used to create a simple cut between the structural members. The **Coped cut** button creates a cut, which takes the shape of the cutting surface.

Cutting member

The **Corner Treatment** window appears.

The **Gap distance** box is used to specify gaps at the corners of the structural members.

You can select the required options from the **Corner Treatment** window and click the green check on the window; the corner treatment will be applied to the selected corner.

The **Alignment** option in the **Settings** section is used to specify the alignment of the structural member about the line segment. Click in the **Alignment** selection box and select the horizontal line; the **Align horizontal axis** and **Align vertical axis** options get active.

The **Align horizontal axis** option aligns the horizontal axis of the beam cross-section with the line segment.

If you want to apply the corner treatment individually, click on the corner point that you want to change.

The **Align vertical axis** option aligns the vertical axis of the beam cross-section with the line segment.

The **Rotation Angle** box allows you to align the structural member at an angle to the line segment.

The **Locate Profile** button allows you to locate the profile of the beam cross-section in the graphics window.

You can change the position of the profile by clicking any another point on the profile.

You can also use the **Mirror Profile** option and mirror the profile about the **Horizontal axis** or **Vertical axis**.

16. After specifying all the settings, click **OK** on the **PropertyManager**.

Notice the two features: **Cut list** and **Weldment** are listed in the **FeatureManager Design Tree**.

17. Save and close the document.

TUTORIAL 2

In this tutorial, you will create the weldment model as shown.

1. Start a new part document.
2. Create the layout sketch as shown.

This layout sketch can be created as a 3D sketch or a combination of 2D and 3D sketches.

You can follow the steps given next to create the layout sketch.

3. On the CommandManager, click **Weldments > 3D Sketch** .
4. On the CommandManager, click **Sketch > Line**.
5. Select the origin point, move the pointer up along the dotted lines, and click.

6. On the CommandManager, click **Sketch > Rectangle drop-down > Corner Rectangle** .
7. Select the end point of the line to define the first corner of the rectangle.
8. Press the Tab key until the rectangle is oriented, as shown.

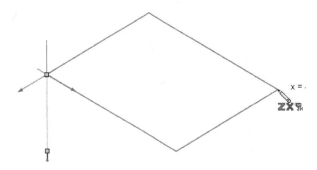

9. Move the pointer and click to create the rectangle.
10. On the CommandManager, click **Sketch > Line**.
11. Select the corner point of the rectangle, as shown.
12. Press the Tab key to switch to the XY plane.
13. Move the pointer the downward and click.

14. Press Esc to deactivate the tool.

275.73, 90°

15. Likewise, create other lines as shown.

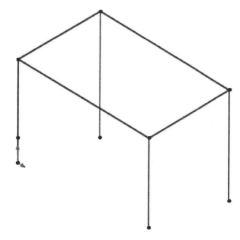

16. Activate the Line tool and select the midpoint of the horizontal line as shown.

17. Press the Tab key to switch to the ZX plane.
18. Select the midpoint of the other horizontal line and press Esc.

296.79, 180°

19. Press the Ctrl key and select all the vertical lines.
20. Click the **Equal** icon on the PropertyManager.
21. Click and drag the corner point of the rectangle and notice that the vertical line length changes.

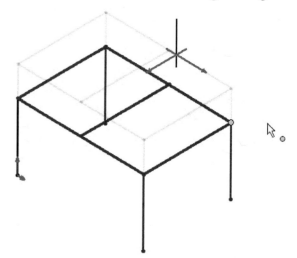

22. Add 300 mm dimension to anyone of the vertical lines.
23. Click and drag the corner of the rectangle as shown. Notice that one side of the rectangle is fixed but the other one is moveable.

24. Press the Ctrl key and click on the corner points of the rectangle, as shown.

25. Click **Along X** [icon] icon on the PropertyManager.
26. Click and drag the corner point of the rectangle, as shown. Notice that the length and width of the rectangle changes.

27. Add dimensions to the length and width of the rectangle. The sketch is fully defined and turned into black.
28. Exit the sketch.

After creating the layout sketch, you need to create the structural members.

Adding Structural members

1. Click the **Structural Member** button on the **Weldment** CommandManager.
2. Select **iso** from the **Standard** drop-down.
3. Select **square tube** from the **Type** drop-down.
4. Select **30X30X2.6** from the **Size** drop-down.
5. Start selecting the line segments of the sketch layout.

Group 3

Note that you can select either the continuous or parallel line segments. If you try to select the non-continuous or parallel segment, you will be not allowed to do so.

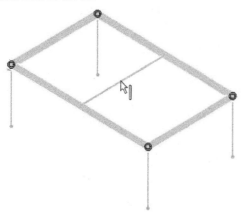

To add structural members to the non-continuous segments, you need to create a new group.

6. Click the **New Group** button below the **Groups** selection box and select the line segments.

Group 2

Note that the order in which the structural members are created defines the members that will be trimmed. The structural members that are crossing already created members will be trimmed.

7. Click the **OK** button on the PropertyManager to accept the selection.
8. In the FeatureManager Design Tree, click on the **3DSketch** and select **Edit Sketch**.
9. Draw a line connecting the midpoints of the horizontal lines, as shown.

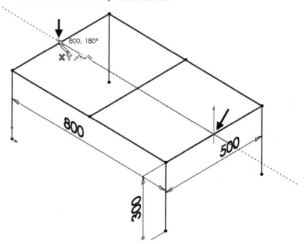

10. Exit the sketch.
11. Activate the **Structural Member** tool.
12. Select **iso** from the **Standard** drop-down.
13. Select **square tube** from the **Type** drop-down.
14. Select **30X30X2.6** from the **Size** drop-down.
15. Select the line segment and create a structural member, as shown.

Trimming the Structural Members

The structural members will be trimmed automatically if you have created them as a single instance. However, if you have created the structural members by activating the **Structural Member** tool several times, they will not be trimmed automatically. You need to trim those members by using the **Trim/Extend** tool.

1. To trim the structural members, click the **Trim/Extend** button on the **Weldments** CommandManager.

2. Select the structural member, as shown.

3. Select the **Bodies** option from the **Trimming Boundary** section.
4. Click in the **Trimming Boundary** selection box and select the horizontal member, as shown.

5. Click the **Simple cut between bodies** button.

6. Click **OK**. The structural member will be trimmed.

7. Again, activate the **Trim/Extend** tool.
8. Select the body to be trimmed, as shown.
9. Click in the selection box in the **Trimming Boundary** section.
10. Select the structural member intersecting first body.

11. Click the **End Miter** icon on the PropertyManager. The two structural members will be trimmed to form a mitered corner.

12. Click the **End Butt1** icon.

13. Click the **End Butt2** icon.

14. Click the **End Trim** icon on the PropertyManager and select the **Face/plane** option.

15. Select the side faces of the intersecting structural members.

16. Click **OK** to trim the structural member.

Creating Gussets

Gussets are plates used to reinforce corners. Gussets can be created between any two faces that intersect at an angle between 0 and 180 degrees.

1. To create a gusset, click the **Gusset** button on the **Weldments** CommandManager.

2. Select the two faces to join with a gusset, as shown.

The gusset can be created in a triangular or polygonal shape.

3. Select the **Triangular Profile** icon from the **Profile** section.

The size of the gusset can be controlled by the options available in the **Profile** section. Each option

corresponds to the dimension shown on the profile button.

4. Enter the values as shown.

The **Chamfer** button in the **Profile** section allows you to add a chamfer to the inside edge of the gusset.

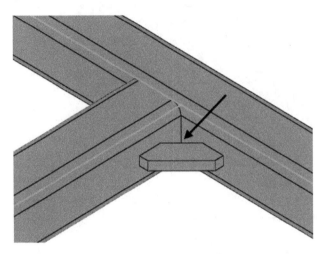

The thickness of the gusset can be specified using the thickness buttons and the **Gusset Thickness** edit box.

5. Click the **Both Sides** icon and enter 6 in the **Gusset Thickness** box.

The location of the gussets can be defined by using the options in the **Location** section.

If you want to define the gusset at an offset from the location, check the **Offset** option and enter the offset value in the **Offset Value** box.

6. Click the **Mid Point** button in the **Location** section.
7. Click **OK** to create the gusset.

You can use the **Extruded Boos/Base** tool to create gussets with custom shapes and sizes.

Creating Base Plates

1. On the CommandManager, click **Weldments > Extruded Boss/Base** .
2. Zoom and rotate the model to display the bottom face of the front left column.
3. Select the bottom face of the column.

4. On the **Sketch** tab, click **Rectangle drop-down >**

Center Rectangle.

5. Select the origin point and create a centered rectangle.

6. Exit the sketch.
7. Leave the **Merge result** option unchecked.
8. Type-in 5 in the **Depth** box extrude the sketch downwards.

Mirroring Gussets and Base plates

1. On the CommandManager, click **Weldments >**

Reference Geometry > Plane .
2. Select the Top plane from the FeatureManager Design Tree.

3. Select the two points from the layout sketch, as shown.

4. Click **OK** on the PropertyManager.
5. On the CommandManager, click **Features > Mirror** .
6. Select the new plane to define the mirror plane.
7. On the PropertyManager, expand the **Bodies to Mirror** section.
8. Select the gusset and base plate, and then click **OK**.

10. Activate the **Plane** tool, and select the Front plane and the point, as shown.

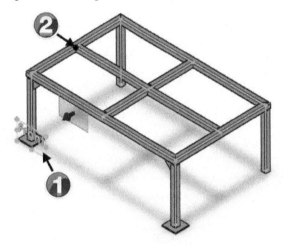

11. Mirror the base plates and gusset bodies about the new plane.

9. Hide the plane.

Creating Fillet Beads

You can create fillet beads to add weld information to the model. The **Fillet Bead** is the older SolidWorks tool. The **Weld Bead** tool can be used instead of this tool for performance and new enhancements. However, this tool is explained to know its basic functionality.

1. To create a fillet bead, click **Insert > Weldments > Fillet Bead** from the Menu bar.

You can create three types of fillet beads: **Full Length**, **Intermittent** and **Staggered**.

2. Select **Full Length** from the drop-down available in the **Arrow Side** section.
3. Enter **3** in the **Fillet size** box.

Next, you need to select intersecting faces to create a fillet weld between then.

4. Zoom to base plate of the front right column.
5. Select the top face of the base plate.
6. Click in the **Face set 2** selection box and select a face of the column, as shown.

7. Make sure that the **Tangent Propagation** option is checked. You will notice that the bead is created around the structural member.
8. Leave the **Add weld symbol** option checked.
9. Click **OK** to create the fillet bead.

Creating Weld Beads

You can add weld beads to parts, assemblies or multi-body parts.

1. To add a weld bead, click the **Weld Bead** button on the **Weldments** CommandManager.
2. Zoom to the base plate of the front left column.
3. Select the top face of the base plate.
4. Select the faces of the column, as shown.

5. Check the **Tangent Propagation** option and notice that all the tangent edges are selected. The **All round** option also gives the same result.

6. Uncheck the **Tangent Propagation** option and

select the **Both sides** option. The opposite edge also is selected.

The **Both sides** option will be more useful while adding a weld to the gussets or plates.

7. Select the **Selection** option and select faces, as shown.

8. Check the **Form/To Length** option on the

PropertyManager. Notice two arrows at the start and ends of the weld path.

9. Type-in 10 in the **Start point** box and notice that the start point is offset by 10 mm. In addition, the weld length is updated, automatically.

10. Click the **Reverse Direction** icon next to the **Start point** box. The start and ends of the weld are reversed.

You can also check the **Intermittent Weld** option to create gaps along the weld.

You can create an intermittent weld by specifying the **Gap and weld length** or **Pitch and weld length**.

11. Enter 3 in the **Bead Size** box
12. Click the **Define Weld Symbol** button in the **Settings** section.
13. Click the **Weld Symbol** button on the top of the leader.
14. Select the **Fillet** ◺ symbol from the flyout.

You can also click **More Symbols** on the flyout to open the **Symbol library** dialog. You can select symbols from a wide range of categories. Click **OK** after selecting the desired symbol.

15. Click **OK** on the dialog. Notice the weld symbol.

You can create multiple weld paths in a single instance.

16. Click the **New Weld Path** button in the **Weld Path** section.

Now, you need to define the weld path. You can define the weld path by selecting faces from the

model or using the **Smart Weld Selection Tool** .

17. Click **Smart Weld Selection Tool** in the **Weld Path** section.

18. Click and drag the pointer crossing the edges, as shown. The edges are selected as soon as you release the pointer.

Notice that the offset is applied to the new weld path as well. You can uncheck the **From/To Length** option to remove the offset for the selected weld path.

19. Click **OK** on the Property Manager. The weld is added to the model.

20. Activate the **Weld Bead** tool and **Weld Path**

under the **Settings** section on the PropertyManager.

21. Zoom to the base plate of the back right column.

22. Click the right mouse button on the horizontal edge of the column and select **Select Tangency**. All the tangentially connected edges are selected.

23. Leave the settings on the PropertyManager and click **OK**.

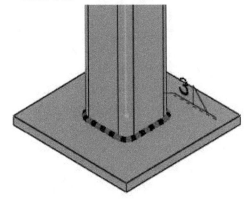

24. Likewise, add the weld bead to the other column.

Notice that there is a **Weld Folder** in the FeatureManager Design Tree. It is added to the FeatureManager Design Tree as you create weld beads.

On expanding this folder, you can see the welds that are created.

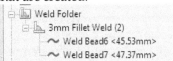

You can edit the properties of the weld by right clicking on it and selecting **Properties**.

The **Weld Bead Properties** dialog appears.

You can change the properties of the weld bead in this dialog. Note that weld beads are for representation same as cosmetic thread. They do not have any mass properties. When you have calculated the total mass of the model, the mass of the weld bead is excluded from model. You can add the **Total Weld Mass** value to the total mass of the model.

To edit a weld bead, right click on it and select **Edit Feature**.

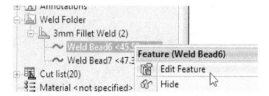

TUTORIAL 3 (Creating End Caps)

End caps are used to close the open ends of the structural members. Note that you can only apply end caps to structural members having linear edges. You cannot apply them to round tubes.

1. Start a new part document and create the model, as shown.

2. To create an end cap, click the **End Cap** button on the **Weldments** Command Manager.

3. Select the end face of the structural member, as shown.

4. Click the **Outward** icon under the **Thickness direction** section. The preview of the end cap appears on the outer face.

5. Click the **Inward** icon under the **Thickness direction** section. The preview of the end cap appears inside the structural member. However, it will be created on the end face of the member. The inward end cap means that it will be created inside the original length of the structural member.

6. Click the **Internal** icon under the **Thickness direction** section. The preview of the end cap appears inside the structural member. You can further inset the end cap by entering a value in the **Inset Distance** box.

7. Click the **Outward** icon and specify the **Thickness** as **3**.

The size of the end cap can be defined using the options in the **Offset** section.

8. Select **Offset value** and enter 5 in the Offset value box. The size of the end cap is reduced by 5 mm. You can click the **Reverse Direction** icon to increase the end cap size.

11. Check the **Corner Treatment** option to apply chamfer or fillet the end cap corners.
12. Select **Chamfer** and type-in 3 in the **Chamfer Distance** box.

13. Select **Fillet** and type-in 3 in the **Fillet Radius** box.

9. Select **Thickness Ratio** and enter 1 in the **Thickness Ratio** box. The size of the end cap is reduced by the weldment thickness value.

14. Click **OK** to create the end cap.

10. Change the **Thickness Ratio** to 0.5. The size of the weldment is reduced by the half of the weldment thickness value.

TUTORIAL 4 (Working with Cut lists)

1. Open the Tutorial 2 file.

Cut lists are used to document weldment designs. They contain the information about the type of structural members, the lengths of the individual members and any other information necessary to manufacture a weldment. SolidWorks automatically creates a cut list as you design a weldment. As soon as a weldment is added, the **Cut list** folder is added to the FeatureManager Design Tree.

You will notice that the **Solid Bodies** folder is missing. When a structural member is added to the part making it a weldment, the **Solid Bodies** folder is replaced with the **Cut list** folder. As you continue to add weldment features, these features are listed individually within the **Cut list** folder.

The Cut list is generated and updated automatically as the **Update automatically** option is selected. You can click the right mouse button on the Cut list and deselect this option.

You can see that several subfolders are created within the **Cut list** folder. All the like items such as plates, end caps, and gussets are grouped into individual subfolders. Structural Members and weldment components are represented by the weld symbol . Other items are listed in normal folders. You can also reorder these folders by clicking and dragging them.

You can also exclude items from the Cut list by right-clicking on them and selecting **Exclude from cut list**.

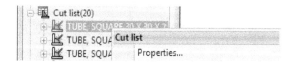

You can also include the excluded items by right-clicking and selecting **Include in cut list**. It is recommended that you make changes to the **Cut list** only after completing the weldment design. If you add any additional members to the model, you will lose all of the changes made to the Cut list order.

Adding Cut list to the Weldment Drawing

1. Create a drawing by selecting **New > Make Drawing from Part/Assembly**.

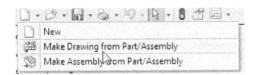

2. Select **Drawing** and click **OK**.
3. In the FeatureManager Design Tree, click the right mouse button on **Sheet 1** and select **Properties**.
4. Select **A2 (ISO)** from the **Sheet Format/Size** section and click **OK**.
5. Place the Isometric view on the drawing sheet.

6. Click **Annotation > Tables > Weldment Cut list** on the CommandManager.

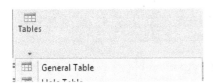

7. Select the view from the drawing sheet. The **Weldment Cut list** PropertyManager appears. The options in this PropertyManager are similar to the **Bill of Materials** one.

8. Click **OK** on the Property Manager and place the cut list table on the drawing sheet.

ITEM NO.	QTY.	DESCRIPTION	LENGTH
1	2	TUBE, SQUARE 1.18 X 1.18 X 0.10	32.68
2	2	TUBE, SQUARE 1.18 X 1.18 X 0.10	20.87
3	4	TUBE, SQUARE 1.18 X 1.18 X 0.10	11.22
4	1	TUBE, SQUARE 1.18 X 1.18 X 0.10	30.31
5	2	TUBE, SQUARE 1.18 X 1.18 X 0.10	8.66
6	4		
7	4		

The **Description** and **Length** may or may not be populated in the cut list. It depends on the type of weldment. The **Description** and **Length** of the structural members are automatically populated. Notice that the **Description** and **Length** of the members such as gussets, base plates, and end caps are not populated automatically. To know about the members that are not populated, you need to add balloons to the model view.

9. On the CommandManager, click **Annotation > Auto Balloon**.
10. Click **OK**. Notice that the gussets and base plate are annotated with the 6 and 7 number balloons.

You need to populate these properties manually. To do so, you need to switch to the part document and add properties to these members.

11. Open the part document of the weldment.
12. Expand the **Cut list** folder in the **FeatureManager Design Tree**.

13. Right-click on the **Cut-list-Item6** subfolder under the Cut list folder and select **Properties**; the **Cut list Properties** dialog appears.

14. In the **Cut list Properties** dialog, enter **DESCRIPTION** in the **Property Value** field and **Gusset** in the **Value/Text Expression** field.

	Property Name	Type		Value / Text Expression	
1	MATERIAL	Text	▼	"SW-Material@@@Cut-Item6@Tutorial 2.SL	
2	QUANTITY	Text	▼	"QUANTITY@@@Cut-Item6@Tutorial 2.SLDP	
3	Description ←	Text	▼	Gusset ←	▼
4	<Type a new proper		▼		

15. Click the **Cut-list-Item7** folder and enter **DESCRIPTION** in the **Property Value** field and **Base Plate** in the **Value/Text Expression** field.

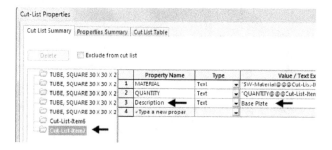

16. Click **OK**.
17. Switch to the Drawing document of the weldment. Notice that the **Description** column is populated in the Cut list table.

Adding Columns to the Cut list table

You can add more columns to the cut list table and save it as a template for the later use.

1. Place the pointer on the table and notice that row and column headers.
2. Click the right mouse button on the right most column and click **Insert > Column Right**.
3. Enter **Weight** in the **Title** box and click **OK**.
4. Open the part document of the weldment.
5. In the FeatureManager Design Tree, click the right mouse button on the Gusset folder and select **Properties**.
6. On the **Cut list Properties** dialog, enter **Weight** in the **Property Value** field and **48** in the **Value/Text Expression** field.

	Property Name	Type		Value / Text Expression	
1	MATERIAL	Text	▼	"SW-Material@@@Gusset<26>@Tutorial 2.SLD	Pla
2	QUANTITY	Text	▼	"QUANTITY@@@Gusset<26>@Tutorial 2.SLDPRT	1
3	Description	Text	▼	Gusset	Gu
4	Weight ←	Number	▼	48 ←	▼
5	<Type a new proper		▼		

7. Click **OK**. Notice that the value is not updated in the cut list table.
8. Click in the Weight column header.
9. On the PropertyManager, select **Cut list item property**, and select **Weight** from the drop-down menu.
10. Click the green check to update the table.

ITEM NO.	QTY.	DESCRIPTION	LENGTH	Weight
1	2	TUBE, SQUARE 1.18 X 1.18 X 0.10	32.68	
2	2	TUBE, SQUARE 1.18 X 1.18 X 0.10	20.87	
3	4	TUBE, SQUARE 1.18 X 1.18 X 0.10	11.22	
4	1	TUBE, SQUARE 1.18 X 1.18 X 0.10	30.31	
5	2	TUBE, SQUARE 1.18 X 1.18 X 0.10	8.66	
6	4	Gusset	→	48
7	4	Base Plate		

11. To save the cut list table as a template, right-click on the table and select **Save As**.

Creating Bounding box

Bounding box is the smallest box around a weldment. It gives you an idea about the weldment dimensions. You can use the bounding box to add some properties to the Cut list, automatically.

1. Open the part document of the weldment model.

2. In the FeatureManager Design Tree, expand the Cut list folder.
3. Click the right mouse button on the **Gusset** folder and select **Create Bounding Box**.
4. Expand the Gusset folder and notice a 3D sketch inside it.

5. Click on the 3D sketch and notice a dotted box around the gusset.

6. Click the right mouse button on the Gusset folder and select **Properties**. Notice the thickness, width, length, and volume properties on the **Cut list Properties** dialog.
7. Click **OK** to close the dialog.

You can edit or delete the bounding box by simply clicking the right mouse button on the folder and selecting **Edit Bounding Box** or **Delete Bounding Box**.

Adding a Weld table to the Weldment Drawing

You can show the weld beads or fillet beads of a weldment in a drawing document. You can show them in the form of a Weld table in the drawing.

1. To add a weld table, click **Insert > Tables > Weld Table** on the Menu bar.

2. Select the Isometric view from the drawing.
3. Click **OK** on the Property Manager.
4. Place the weld table on the drawing sheet.

ITEM NO.	WELD SIZE	SYMBOL	WELD LENGTH	WELD MATERIAL	QTY.
1	3	△	1.79		1
2	3	△	1.86		1
3	3	△	4.37		2

You can also add weld symbols and other annotations to the model view on the drawing.

Adding a Weld Symbols

1. To add weld symbols or other annotations, click **Annotation > Model Items** on the Command Manager;
2. On the **Model Items** Property Manager, set the **Source** to **Entire model**.
3. Deselect the **Marked for drawing** icon.
4. Select the icons from the **Annotations** section, as shown.
5. Click **OK**. The annotations are displayed on the model view.

6. Save the Part document and the drawing document.

Creating Sub Weldments

You can break down a weldment into sub weldments to make it easy to manage them.

1. Open a Part document created in Tutorial 2.
2. Right click on the Command Manager and select **Selection Filter**. The **Selection Filter** toolbar appears at the bottom.

   - Render Tools
   - Screen Capture
   - Selection Filter
   - Sheet Metal

3. Click the **Filter Solid bodies** button on the **Selection Filter** toolbar.

*Isometric

4. Press the Ctrl key and select the structural members as shown.

---

5. Right-click and select **Create Sub-Weldment**.
6. Expand the **Cut list** folder in the FeatureManager Design Tree.

You will notice a new folder under the cut list folder.

7. Open the drawing document of the weldments model. Place the cut list table on the drawing sheet.

ITEM NO.	QTY.	DESCRIPTION	LENGTH	Weight
1	1			
1	4	TUBE, SQUARE 1.18 X 1.18 X 0.10	11.22	
3	4			48
4	4	Base Plate		

You will notice that the **Description** and **Length** values are empty in the cut list. This is because sub weldments are not recognized as weldment parts. You need to save the sub weldments as a separate weldment part.

8. Switch to the part document.
9. Press the Ctrl key and select the structural members as shown.

10. Click the right mouse button and select **Insert into New Part**.
11. On the PropertyManager, check the **Cut list properties** to option and select **Cut list properties**. This option allows you to insert the cut list table into the drawing.
12. Click **OK** on the PropertyManager.
13. Save the file as Tutorial 2-Sub-weldment1.

18. Create a drawing by selecting **New > Make Drawing from Part/Assembly**.

14. Insert the isometric view and cut list table into the drawing.

15. Save it as a separate part file.

TUTORIAL 5 (Creating Custom Profiles for structural members)

If you want to create a structural member using a profile that is not available in SolidWorks, you can create a custom profile.

1. Run SolidWorks as administrator.
2. Open a new Part document.
3. Create a sketch as shown in figure.

4. Exit the sketch.
5. On the Quick Access Toolbar, click the **Options** icon.
6. On the **System Options** dialog, click **File Locations** in the tree.
7. Select **Weldment Profiles** from the **Show folders for** drop-down.
8. See the location of the weldment profiles and click **OK**.
9. Select the sketch from the FeatureManager Design Tree.
10. Click **File > Save As** on the Menu bar; the **Save As** dialog appears.
11. On this dialog, set the **Save as type** as **Lib Feat Part (*.sldlfp).**
12. Browse to the location of the weldment profiles.
13. Create the **Custom Profiles** folder.

14. Create a sub folder with the name **C-Shape** in the **Custom Profiles** folder.
15. Save the file in the C-Shape as C120.
16. Open a new Part document and create a sketch as shown in figure.

17. Exit the sketch.
18. Click **Weldments > Structural Member** on the Command Manager.
19. On the Property Manager, make the selections as shown in figure.

20. Select the line segments from the sketch. The structural members are created.

You can also click the **Locate Profile** button and change the position of the profile.

21. Click **OK**.

22. Save the file.

Chapter 13: DimXpert

Geometric Dimensioning and Tolerancing

During the manufacturing process, the accuracy of a part is an important factor. However, it is impossible to manufacture a part with the exact dimensions. Therefore, while applying dimensions to a drawing you need to provide some dimensional tolerances, which lie within acceptable limits. The following figure shows an example of dimensional tolerances applied to the drawing.

The dimensional tolerances help you to manufacture the component within a specific size range. However, the dimensional tolerances are not sufficient for manufacturing a component. You must give tolerance values to its shape, orientation and position as well. The following figure shows a note, which is used to explain the tolerance value given to the shape of the object.

Providing a note in a drawing may be confusing. To avoid this, we use Geometric Dimensioning and Tolerancing (GD&T) symbols to specify the tolerance values to shape, orientation and position of a component. The following figure shows the same example represented by using the GD&T symbols. In this figure, the vertical face to which the tolerance frame is connected, must be within two parallel planes 0.08 apart and perpendicular to the datum reference (horizontal plane).

Providing GD&T in 2D drawings is common and well known method. However, you can provide GD&T information to 3D models as well. The DimXpert tools help you to add GD&T information to the 3D models based on the universal standards such as ASME Y14.41 – 2003 and ISO 16792 : 2006. However, you can add GD&T information based on your custom standard as well.

In this chapter, you will learn to use **DimXpert** tools to add GD&T information to parts. There are many ways to add GD&T information and full-define the parts and assemblies. There are few methods explained in this chapter but you need to use a method, which is most suitable to your design.

The DimXpert tools are available on the **DimXpert** Command Manager. If the **DimXpert** CommandManager is not displayed by default, you can customize it. Right click on any of the tabs of the CommandManager and select **DimXpert** from the shortcut menu.

TUTORIAL 1 (Auto Dimension Scheme)

This tutorial teaches you to apply tolerances using the **Auto Dimension Scheme** tool. This tool automates the process of adding dimensions and tolerances to the 3D model.

1. Download the DimXpert part files from the Companion website and open the Tutorial 1 file.
2. On the Quick Access Toolbar, click the **Options** icon to open the **System Options** dialog.
3. Click the **Document Properties** tab and select **Drafting Standard** from the tree.
4. Set the **Overall drafting standard** to ISO.
5. Click **OK**.
6. On the CommandManager, click **DimXpert >** **Auto Dimension Scheme** .
7. On the PropertyManager, set the **Part type** to

Prismatic. This option is selected for the parts that have planar faces. The **Turned** option can be used for cylindrical shaped parts.

8. Set the **Tolerance type** to **Plus and Minus**.

The **Tolerance type** defines the way in which the features such as holes and cuts are located with reference to datum feature.

The **Plus and Minus** option adds location dimensions with + and – tolerances.

The **Geometric** option uses Geometric Tolerance symbols to represent the positions of features such as holes and cuts. The type of GD&T symbols used will be based on the **Part type**. For example, if you set the **Part type** to **Prismatic**, the Position symbol will be used to locate a hole. However, if the **Part type** is set to **Turned**, the Circular Runout symbol will be used to position a hole.

Next, you need to define the datum features. A datum is used as a reference to measure the location, shape, and size of a feature. A datum can be a surface, point, or axis.

9. On the PropertyManager, click in the **Primary Datum** selection box and select the top face of the geometry.
10. Click in the **Secondary Datum** selection box and select the front face of the geometry.
11. Click in the **Tertiary Datum** selection box and select the right face.

12. Under the **Scope** section, select **All features**.
13. Check all the options in the **Feature Filters** section and click **OK**.

Notice the dimensions added to the 3D geometry.
They all have + and – tolerances.

14. Click the **DimXpertManager** tab and notice the
    features listed in it. The **Auto Dimension
    Scheme** tool recognizes and lists the features to
    be manufactured, automatically.

Notice that the Extruded Cut feature is recognized
as a Slot feature. The DimXpert recognizes the
features based on the manufacturing language.

15. Right click on the part in the DimXpertManager
    tree and select **Delete**.

16. Click **Yes** on the **SOLIDWORKS** message to
    delete all the dimensions and tolerances.
17. On the DimXpertManager tree, click the **Auto
    Dimension Scheme** icon.
18. Set the **Tolerance type** to **Geometric**.
19. Select the primary, secondary, and tertiary
    datums. They are same, as previously selected.
20. Leave the default settings and click **OK**. Notice
    the dimensions and geometric tolerances added
    with reference to the datums.

21. Right click on the part in the DimXpertManager
    tree and select **Delete**.
22. Click **Yes** on the **SOLIDWORKS** message to
    delete all the dimensions and tolerances.
23. Activate the **Auto Dimension Scheme** tool.
24. Select the primary, secondary, and tertiary
    datums. They are same, as previously selected.
25. On the PropertyManager, set the **Scope** to
    Selected features.
26. Select anyone of the holes.
27. Select the Pattern icon on the Selection
    toolbar. The entire pattern is selected.
28. Click **OK** to add dimensions and tolerance to
    the selected features only.

29. Save and close the file.

TUTORIAL 2 (Adding the GD&T Information Manually)

In this tutorial, you will add dimensions and
tolerances manually.

1. Open the Tutorial 2 part file.
2. On the CommandManager, click **DimXpert >
   Datum** .

3. On the PropertyManager, type **A** in the **Label** box under the **Label Settings** section.
4. Select the front face of the geometry.
5. Move the pointer and click to position the datum.

6. Likewise, define the datum B and C, and click **OK**.

Notice the three plane features in the DimXpertManager tree.

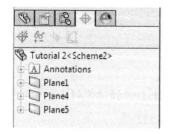

You can click and drag the datum or its origin point.

You can change the orientation of the datum by clicking the right mouse button on it and selecting **Select Annotation View**. Select a new annotation view from the popup menu. If you select Top annotation view, the orientation of the datum will be changed to Top.

If you select the **By Selection** option, then datum is oriented to the selected plane.

7. On the CommandManager, click the **Show Tolerance Status** icon. Notice that the datum faces are highlighted in green, which means that they are fully-defined.

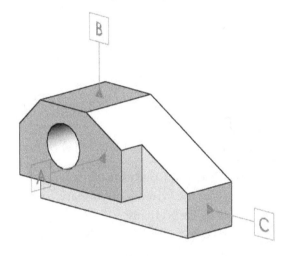

Now, you need to fully-define all other faces by adding dimensions and tolerances.

Adding Size Dimensions

You add size dimensions to the geometry to provide the manufacturing information. These dimensions do not control the geometry. Instead, they are controlled by the size of the geometry.

1. On the CommandManager, click **DimXpert > Size Dimension** .
2. Select the hole and place the dimension.

Notice the tolerance values added to the dimension. This are the default tolerance values set on the **System Options** dialog. You can change the tolerance value on the **System Options** dialog. You can also change the tolerance on the **Tolerance/Precision** section of the **DimXpert** PropertyManager.

In addition, if you select a single hole from the geometry, all the holes of same size will be selected, automatically and the hole count will added to the dimension.

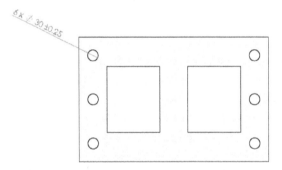

3. Click **OK** on the DimXpert PropertyManager.
4. Click the **Show Tolerance Status** icon on the DimXpertManager. Notice that the hole is highlighted in yellow, which means that is it under constrained.

Adding Location Dimensions

You add location dimensions to a feature with reference to a datum.

1. On the CommandManager, click **DimXpert > Location Dimension** .

2. Rotate the model and select its left vertical face.
3. Select the hole and position the dimension, as shown.

On the **DimXpert** PropertyManager, the **Tolerance Feature** and **Origin Feature** are displayed in the **Reference Features** section. You can swap these features by clicking the **Swap Features** icon.

You can also change the tolerance value in the **Tolerance/Precision** section.

4. Add a dimension between the bottom face and hole.

5. Select the lower horizontal edge of the geometry and notice the faces perpendicular to the edge are highlighted.
6. Position the dimension and click **OK** on the PropertyManager.

Adding Geometric Tolerances

1. On the CommandManager, click **DimXpert > Geometric Tolerance** .

2. On the Properties dialog, select Position ⊕ from the **Symbol** drop-down.
3. Type 0.02 in the **Tolerance 1** box and click the **Maximum Material Condition** icon.
4. Type A, B, C in the **Primary**, **Secondary**, and **Tertiary** boxes, respectively.
5. Select the hole and position the tolerance frame. The SOLIDWORKS message appears showing that tolerance over constrains the part.
6. Click **OK** to add the tolerance.
7. Click **OK** on the **Properties** dialog and delete the location dimensions, as shown.

8. Add three tolerance frames to the faces, as shown.

Adding other dimensions to Fully-define the part

1. On the CommandManager, click **Location Dimension** and add dimensions, as shown.

2. Activate the **Location Dimension** tool and click the left vertical face of the geometry.

3. Click the **Create Intersection Line** icon on the Selection toolbar.

4. Select the inclined face and click **OK**.

5. Select the top face of the geometry and position the dimension.

6. On the PropertyManager, click the **Swap Features** icon to change the origin feature.

7. Click **Close Dialog**.

8. Click the **Show Tolerance Status** icon and notice that the inclined face is highlighted in yellow.

In addition, notice that the other inclined is not fully-defined. You need to add dimensions to fully-define these two faces.

9. Activate the **Location Dimension** tool and click the top face of the geometry.

10. Click the **Create Intersection Line** icon on the Selection toolbar.

11. Select the left inclined face and click **OK**.

12. Select the C datum face and position the dimension.

13. On the PropertyManager, click the **Swap Features** icon to change the origin feature.

14. Click **Close Dialog**.

15. Likewise, add the angle and linear dimensions, as shown.

16. Save and close the file.

TUTORIAL 3 (Using the DimXpert Annotations in drawings)

1. Open the Tutorial 2 part file.

2. On the Quick Access Toolbar, click **New > Make Drawing from Part/Assembly**.

3. Select **A3(ISO)** from the **Sheet Format/Size** dialog and click **OK**.

4. On the **View Palette**, check the **Import Annotations** and **DimXpert Annotations** options.

5. Drag the Front view from the **View Palette** onto the drawing sheet.

6. Click **Close Dialog** on the **Projected View** PropertyManager.

7. Likewise, drag the Right and Isometric views.

8. Adjust the dimensions by dragging them.

9. Save and close the drawing file.

TUTORIAL 4 (Pattern Feature)

1. Open the Tutorial 4 part file.

2. On the CommandManager, click **DimXpert > Pattern Feature** .

3. On the PropertyManager, select **Linked Patterns**.

4. Select anyone of the holes of the curve pattern.

5. Click **OK** and notice the Hole Pattern in the DimXpertManager.

6. Change the instant count of the curve pattern to 10. Notice that the Hole Pattern in the DimXpertManager is also updated.
7. Activate the **Pattern Feature** command and select anyone of the large holes.

8. The other hole of the same size is selected, automatically. In addition, the **Manual Patterns** option is active as the holes are created as two separate instances. The **Find all same face** option selects all the features of same size.
9. Click **OK**. The Hole Pattern appears in the DimXpertManager Tree.

10. Activate the **Pattern Feature** command and select **Collection**.
11. Select the side faces of the geometry.

12. The Collection feature appears in the DimXpertManager Tree. All the faces inside the Collection feature as a single DimXpert feature. You can add an annotation to all the faces of the collection feature at a time.

TUTORIAL 5 (DimXpert Options)

1. Start a new Part document.
2. On the Quick Access Toolbar, click **Options** to the **System Options** dialog.
3. Click the **Document Properties** tab and select **Drafting Standard** from the tree.
4. Set the **Overall drafting standard** to **ISO**.
5. Click **DimXpert** in the tree.

The **Method** is set to **General Tolerance**. You can define the **Tolerance class** as Fine, Medium, Coarse, or Very Coarse.

The **Block Tolerance** method can be used, if you are using the ANSI drafting standard. You can define the decimal values for the length and angle dimensions in the **Block tolerance** section.

6. Click **Size Dimension** in the tree.

On this page, you can define the default tolerance values to be added to the DimXpert size dimensions. You can specify three types of the tolerances (Symmetric, Bilateral, and General) for various types of features. The tolerances can be specified separately for each feature.

7. Click **Location Dimension** in the tree.

On this page, you can define the default tolerance values for the location dimensions. In addition, you can set the type of the dimensions to be added to inclined planes using the **Auto Dimension Scheme**.

8. Click **Chain Dimension** in the tree.

On this page, you can define the dimensioning method for holes and pockets using the **Auto Dimension Scheme**. In addition, you can define the tolerances for patterns.

9. Click **Geometric Tolerance** in the tree.

This page allows you to set the default options for geometric tolerances to be added using the **Auto Dimension Scheme**.

Likewise, you can set the default width and tolerance settings on the **Chamfer Control** page.

10. Click **Display Options** on the tree.

This page allows you to control the way the dimensions and tolerances are displayed using the **Auto Dimension Scheme**. In addition, you can control the redundant dimensions and tolerances using **Eliminate duplicates** and **Show instance count** options.

11. Click **OK** to close the dialog.

Chapter 14: Appearances and Rendering

In this chapter, you will:

- Add Appearances and Textures to the model
- Apply Backgrounds and Scenes to the model
- Render Images
- Add Cameras and Lights
- Create Walkthroughs
- Add Decals

TUTORIAL 1 (Adding Appearances to the Complete Part)

1. Download the Appearances and Rendering part files from the Companion website and open the Tutorial 1 file.
2. On the View Toolbar, click the **Edit Appearance** icon.

You can also right click on the part in the FeatureManager Design Tree and select **Appearances > Tutorial 1**.

3. Click the **Basic** tab on the PropertyManager. Notice that Tutorial 1.SLDPRT is listed in the **Selected Geometry** section. You can use the **Select Part**, **Select Faces**, **Select Surfaces**, **Select Bodies**, and **Select Features** icons to select different types of geometry.
4. Leave the entire part as Selected Geometry in the PropertyManager.

5. Click the **Appearances, Scenes, and Decals** tab on the Task pane.
6. On the Task pane, click **Appearances (color) > Metal > Aluminum**. Notice the various types of Aluminum listed on the lower portion of the Task pane.
7. Select **blue anodized aluminum** from the Task pane.

blue anodized aluminum

aluminum treadplate

8. Click **OK** on the PropertyManager to apply the selected material to whole part.

9. Click the **DisplayManager** tab and notice that the material is added to the Appearances tree.
10. Expand **blue anodized aluminum** and notice that the material is attached to the entire part geometry.

11. Right click on the appearance and select **Edit Appearance**.
12. On the Task pane, click **Appearances (color) > Metal > Copper**. Notice the various types of Copper listed on the lower portion of the Task pane.
13. Select **brushed copper** from the Task pane and click **OK**.

Also, notice the brushed copper on the **DisplayManager**.

14. Right click on **brushed copper** and select **Remove Appearance** (or) select the appearance and press Delete (or) right on the appearance and select Edit Appearance, and then click **Remove Appearance** on the **Selected Geometry** section.

The appearance is removed from the geometry.

TUTORIAL 2 (Adding Appearances to Faces, Surfaces, and Features)

SolidWorks allows you to apply different appearances on a single part. For example, you can display some faces of the geometry differently from others. To add different appearances to the part geometry, you need to understand hierarchy in which the appearances are added. For example, if you add an appearance to the entire part, and then add a different appearance to a part feature, the feature appearance will be added on top of the part appearance. If you add a new appearance to a face of the feature, the face appearance will be added on top of the feature appearance.

1. Open the Tutorial 2 part file.

Now, you need to add appearance to the Boss-Extrude feature, as shown.

2. Right click on the **Boss-Extrude** feature and select **Appearances > Boss-Extrude**.

Notice the Boss-Extrude feature in the **Selected Geometry** section.

15. On the Task pane, click **Appearances (color) > Metal > Bronze**. Notice the various types of Bronze listed on the lower portion of the Task pane.
16. Select **cast bronze** from the Task pane and click **OK**.

Notice the **cast bronze** on the **DisplayManager**. It is attached to the Boss-Extrude feature

17. Press the Ctrl key and select the faces of the geometry, as shown.

18. On the DisplayManager, right click on the **cast bronze** appearance and select **Attach To Selection**. The appearance is attached to the selected faces.

You can also use the Copy and Paste options to apply appearance to multiple features/faces of the geometry.

19. Click on anyone of the faces with the **cast bronze** appearance, and select **Copy Appearance** 🔧 (or) right click on the **cast bronze** appearance and select **Copy Appearance**.
20. Select the face as shown and click **Paste Appearance**.

21. Click the Boss-Extrude icon on the **Appearance Target Palette**. The **cast bronze** appearance is pasted on the extruded boss.

TUTORIAL 3 (Adding Textures)

Textures are two-dimensional images that are wrapped around a 3D model. The process of adding textures to the 3D model involves selecting an image and mapping it onto the 3D model. As you add a texture, SolidWorks increases or reduces the image size, rotates, and patterns it to completely cover the part geometry.

1. Open the Tutorial 1 file.
2. On the View Toolbar, click the **Edit Appearance** icon.

3. Select **texture** from the Task pane.

color

texture

4. On the PropertyManager, under the **Image** section, click the **Browse** button.
5. Go to *C:\ Program Files \ SolidWorks Corp\ SOLIDWORKS\ data\ Images\ textures\ meta l\ rough.*
6. Select **cast** and click **Open**.

7. On the PropertyManager, click the **Mapping** tab.

The **Mapping** tab has options to select the geometry, and set mapping style and size.

8. On the **Mapping Controls** section, click on the different Mapping styles and notice the appearance on the geometry. Each of the mapping style affects the appearance on the geometry. You can select the Mapping style based on the shape of the geometry.
9. Click on the different **Mapping sizes** and notice the difference.
10. Leave the default options and click **OK**.

TUTORIAL 4 (Texture Mapping options)

1. Start a new part file.
2. Create a box, sphere and cylinder.
3. Apply the loop texture separately to each feature. The location of the texture image is: C:\Program Files\SolidWorks Corp\SOLIDWORKS\data\Images\textures\fabric\loop.jpg

4. Click on the box and select **Edit Appearance > Boss-Extrude**.

5. On the PropertyManager, click the **Advanced** tab, and then click the **Mapping** tab. Notice that the options found in the **Mapping** section are same as the Mapping style options in the **Basic** tab.
6. On the **Mapping** tab, select **Mapping > Surface**. This mapping style arranges the image to fit the surfaces of the geometry.
7. On the **Mapping** section, drag the **Horizontal Location** and **Vertical Location** draggers. Notice that the position of the texture image changes horizontally and vertically.

8. Select **Mapping > Projection** and set the **Projection direction** to XY. The texture image is projected onto the feature in the XY direction.

9.   Set the **Projection direction** to **Current View**.
10. Rotate the model and click the **Update to Current** button. The texture is projected based on the current orientation of the model.

11. Set the **Projection direction** to the **Selected Reference** and select the vertical edge of the box. The image is project along the selected edge.

12. Click **OK** on the PropertyManager.
13. Click on the sphere and select **Edit Appearance > Revolve**.
14. On the PropertyManager, click the **Advanced** tab, and then click the **Mapping** tab.
15. On the **Mapping** tab, select **Mapping > Spherical**. This mapping style arranges the image to fit the surface of a sphere.
16. Drag the **Offset Latitude** and **Offset Longitude** draggers on the **Mapping** section. The position of the rectangle changes.
17. Drag the dotted handles of the rectangle to increase/decrease the size of the texture image.

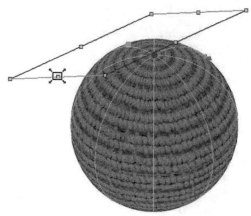

You can also use the **Size/Orientation** options to modify the texture image size and orientation.

The **Fixed aspect ratio** option locks the aspect ratio of the image.

The **Fit width to selection** locks the image width to its current size. You can change only the height of the image.

The **Fit height to selection** locks the image height allowing you to change only its width.

18. Drag the **Rotation** dragger and notice that the image is rotated about the current position of longitude and latitude.

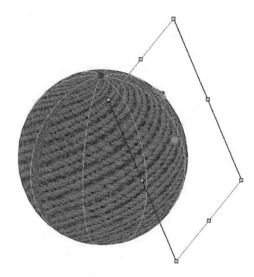

19. Drag the **Axis direction 1** dragger to change its orientation.

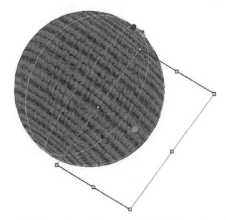

20. Likewise, drag the **Axis direction 2** dragger to change its orientation.

You can use the **Mirror horizontally** or **Mirror vertically** options to mirror the image.

21. Click the **Reset Scale** button to reset image scale to its default value.
22. Click **OK** on the PropertyManager.
23. Click on the cylinder and select **Edit Appearance > Boss-Extrude2**.
24. On the **Mapping** tab, select **Mapping > Cylindrical**. This mapping style arranges the image to fit the surface of a cylinder.
25. Set the **Axis direction** to XY and drag the **About Axis** and **Along Axis** draggers.

26. Click **OK** on the PropertyManager.

Tutorial 5 (Surface Finish)

1. Open the Tutorial 5 file.
2. Apply the **knurl2** texture to the cylindrical face of the geometry. The location of the texture image is C:\Program Files\SolidWorks Corp\SOLIDWORKS\data\Images\textures\m etal\machined
3. The **Mapping Style** is **Surface** and **Mapping Size** is **Big**.

27. Click on the knurled face and select **Edit Appearance > Face**.

28. Click the **Advanced** tab, and then click the **Surface Finish** tab.
29. Select the **Knurled** option from the **Surface Finish** drop-down. You can also select the **From file** option and specify an image file to define the surface finish.
30. Check the **Dynamic help** option.
31. Place the pointer on the **Knurl angle** and **Knurl height cap** boxes, and notice the descriptions.
32. Set the **Knurl angle** and **Knurl height cap** to 90 and 1, respectively.
33. Click **OK**. The knurled surface finish will be visible in the rendered image. SOLIDWORKS will process the bright areas of the texture image as height and the dark areas as depths.

Tutorial 6 (Illumination)

1. Open the Tutorial 5 file.
2. Click on anyone of the face of the geometry and select **Edit Appearance > Revolve**.
3. On the Task Pane, select **Appearance > Metal > Steel**.
4. Select **machined steel** from the lower portion of the Task pane.
5. Click the **Advanced** tab on the PropertyManager.
6. Click the **Illumination** tab and check the **Dynamic help** option. The options on the **Illumination** tab control the illumination of the geometry.
7. Place the pointer on the edit boxes, and notice the descriptions.
8. Modify the values on the **Illumination** tab and notice the change in the graphics window.
9. Click **OK**.

Tutorial 7 (Scenes)

After adding Appearances, a Scene is an important part of the rendering process. An appearance is added to geometry, whereas a Scene added to the SOLIDWORKS environment. A Scene creates a realistic environment in which the model is placed. For example, you can add a road scene to a car model.

1. Open the Tutorial 7 file.

2. Click the DisplayManager tab, right click on Scene, and select **Edit Scene**.
3. Click **Yes** on the **Background Display Setting** dialog.
4. On the Task pane, expand **Scenes** and notice the folders below it.
5. Click on the **Basic Scenes** folder and notice the thumbnails displayed in the browser. The basic scenes have plain or gradient environments and background.

3 Point Beige

3 Point Blue

6. Select 3 Point Beige scene from the browser.
7. Click the middle mouse button and drag the mouse. Notice that the viewpoint changes as you rotate the part.
8. Click the **Studio Scenes** folder. Most of the studio scenes have static backgrounds.
9. Select Reflective Floor Black from the browser.
10. Rotate the model and notice that the background remains static.
11. Click the **Presentation Scenes** folder and select **Factory Background**.
12. Rotate the model and notice that the environment is sphere shaped and enclosed the part completely. You can set the viewpoint at the angle.
13. Click the **Basic Scenes** folder and select **Plain White**. Notice that the background is changed to plain white. However, you can change the background to suite you requirements.
14. On the PropertyManager, select **Background > Color**.
15. Click on the **Background color** box.
16. On the **Color** dialog, select the Yellow color and click **OK**. The background is changed to yellow.

17. On the PropertyManager, select **Background > Gradient**.
18. Click in the **Bottom gradient color** box, select the blue color, and click **OK**. The bottom gradient is changed to blue.

19. On the PropertyManager, select **Background > Image**.
20. Select the Background.jpg and click **Open**.
21. Position the model as shown.

22. On the PropertyManager, select **Background > Use Environment**. The default environment appears as shown.

An environment is a spherical shaped enclosure. The image used in the environment is specially designed and looks similar to the one shown next. The image file types that are commonly used for environments are HDR files and panoramically designed JPEG files.

You can click the **Browse** button and select an image for the environment background.

23. Click **OK** on the PropertyManager.

Tutorial 8 (Rendering using PhotoView 360)

PhotoView 360 is a SolidWorks Add-In, which allows you to create photo-realistic images.

1. Open the Tutorial 8 file.

2. On the Quick Access Toolbar, click **Options > Add-Ins**.
3. On the **Add-Ins** dialog, check the **PhotoView 360** option and click **OK** (or) click the **PhotoView 360** icon on the **SOLIDWORKS Add-Ins** tab of the CommandManager. The **Render Tools** tab is added to the CommandManager.
4. On the CommandManager, click **Render Tools > Edit Appearance** .
5. On the Task pane, select **Appearances > Metal > Aluminum**, and select **polished Aluminum** from the browser.
6. On the PropertyManager, under the **Color** section, click in the **Dominant Color** box and select the light grey color from the **Color** dialog. Click **OK**.
7. Click in the **Secondary Color** box and select white from the **Color** dialog. Click **OK**.
8. Click **OK** on the PropertyManager.
9. On the CommandManager, click **Render Tools > Edit Scene**.
10. On the Task pane, select **Scenes > Presentation Scenes**, and select **Kitchen Background** from the browser.
11. Rotate, zoom, and pan the model to position it, as shown.

12. On the **View** Toolbar, click the **View Orientation** drop-down and deselect the **View Selector** icon.
13. Click the **New View** icon on the **View Orientation** drop-down.
14. Type **Render1** on the **Named View** dialog and click **OK**.
15. Rotate the model to the different orientation.
16. On the **View** Toolbar, click the **View Orientation** drop-down and select **Render1**.

If you are working in the Assembly environment, the **Take snapshot** tool can be used to capture the different view orientations of the model.

17. Click **OK** on the PropertyManager.

Adding Cameras

1. Click the DisplayManager tab, and then click **View Scene, Lights, and Cameras**.
2. Right click on the **Camera** folder and select **Add Camera**.

The PropertyManager appears and it has options to set the camera type, target point, camera position, camera rotation, field of view, and depth of field.

In addition, the graphics window is split in two. You can adjust the camera position in the left window and preview the camera perspective in the right window.

3. On the PropertyManager, set the **Camera Type** to **Aimed at target**. The camera will always show the selected target point regardless of the camera position. The Floating camera type changes the site as you change the camera position and orientation.
4. Zoom out in the left window and notice a camera.

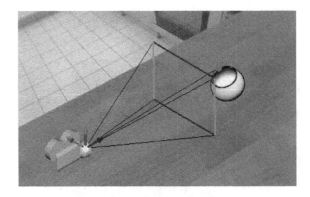

5. Click and drag the red dot attached to the camera. Notice that the target changes as you drag the red dot.
6. Select the outer face of the model to define the target point.
7. Click and drag the yellow dot to change the position of the camera. You can also use the axes of the triad attached to the change the camera position.

Notice that the camera focuses on the target point regardless of its position.

8. Expand the **Camera Rotation** section and drag the **Roll(Twist)** dragger to rotate the camera.
9. Set the **Roll(Twist)** angle to 0 degrees.
10. In the **Field of View** section, select different options from the **Standard lens presets** drop-down and notice the area captured by the camera. You can also drag the **View angle**, **Distance to view rectangle**, and **Height of view rectangle** draggers to adjust the field of view.
11. Check the **Drag Aspect Ratio** option and drag the corner of the view box. The aspect ratio of the field changes dynamically.

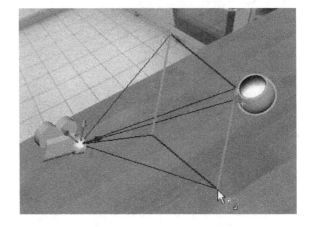

12. Set the **Aspect ratio (width : height)** to **1:1**.

13. Position the camera in such a way that the preview is displayed, as shown.

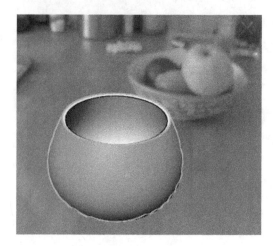

18. Click **OK** on the PropertyManager.
19. In the DisplayManager tree, right click on the Camera and select **Camera View**. The view is locked to the camera.

PhotoView 360 Options

1. On the CommandManager, click **Render Tools > Options** . On the PropertyManager, you can modify the width and height of the image.
2. Check the **Use background aspect ratio** option to avoid the image to be stretched or distorted.
3. Set the **Image Format** to **JPEG**.
4. In the **Render Quality** section, set the **Preview render quality** and **Final render quality** to **Good** and **Best**, respectively. Note that the processing time will increase as you increase the image quality.
5. Leave the other default options and click **OK**.
6. On the View Toolbar, click **View Settings > Perspective** .
7. On the CommandManager, click **Render Tools > Preview Window** . Notice the preview of the rendering.

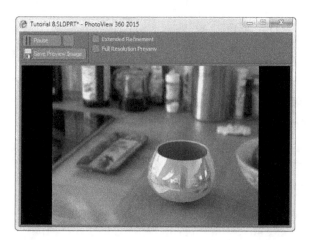

8. On the CommandManager, click **Render Tools > Edit Scene**.
9. On the PropertyManager, click the **PhotoView 360 Lighting** tab.

On this tab, you can adjust the **Background brightness**, **Rendering brightness**, and **Scene reflexivity**. You can also rotate the environment using the **Environment Rotation** dragger.

10. Leave the default settings on the PropertyManager and click **OK**.
11. Click the **Final Render** icon on the **Render Tools** tab. The **Final Render** window appears and rendering is processed. You can click the **Abort** button on the Final Render window, if you want to stop the rendering process.
12. Click the **Statistics** tab to view various statistics of the rendering such as processing time, elapsed time and so on.

After the image is rendered, you can switch between the **Final Color Output** and **Alpha Output** using the **Output** drop-down.

13. Wait until the image is rendered.
14. Click the **Image Processing** tab, and then click the **Advanced Image Processing** button. Notice various image editing options on this tab that are similar to other image processing softwares. You can modify the image using these options.
15. Click the **Compare and Options** tab and notice the options to compare two rendered images.
16. Press and hold the left mouse button on the **Save Image** button, and select **Save Layered Image**.

17. Save the image as Tutorial8.psd file and close the **Final Render** window.

You can use the **Recall Last Render** tool on the **Render Tools** tab to open the last render.

18. Save and close the part file.

Tutorial 9 (Lights)

Lights are very important in rendering a photorealistic image. They can enhance the image to look more realistic by highlighting some portions and creating shadows. You can access the lights on the DisplayManager tree. Click the **DisplayManager** tab, and then click **View Scene, Lights, and Cameras**. Expand the **SOLIDWORKS Lights** folder and notice the default lights available in the SOLIDWORKS environment. Expand the **PhotoView 360 Lights** folder and notice the lights available in PhotoView 360. You can turn ON/OFF lights in PhotoView 360 by right clicking on them and selecting **On in PhotoView 360**.

Editing the Ambient Light

By default, the Ambient light is created is the SOLIDWORKS environment, automatically. The Ambient light falls on the model from all directions.

1. Open the Tutorial 9 file.
2. In the **View Scene, Lights, and Cameras** tree, expand the **SOLIDWORKS Lights** folder, and double click on **Ambient**.
3. On the PropertyManager, click the **Edit Color** button, select the red color from the Color dialog, and click **OK**. Notice that the red light falls on the model.
4. Drag the **Ambient** dragger to change the intensity of the light (or) type-in a value between 0 and 1 in the **Ambient** box.
5. On the PropertyManager, uncheck the **On in SOLIDWORKS** option and notice the difference in the graphics window.
6. Check the **On in SOLIDWORKS** option to turn ON the ambient light.
7. Click **OK** to apply changes to the model.

Tutorial 10 (Working with Directional Lights)

SOLIDWORKS adds a Directional Light to the model, automatically. It is used to highlight a portion of the geometry and display shadows. You can add, delete, move, or adjust the Directional Light.

1. In the **View Scene, Lights, and Cameras** tree, right click on the **SOLIDWORKS Lights** folder, and select **Show Lights**. The directional light appears, as shown.

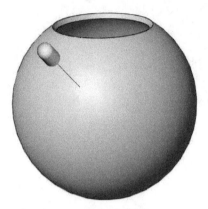

2. Under the **SOLIDWORKS Lights** folder, right click on the **Directional1 light** and select the **Off in SOLIDWORKS** option. The directional light is turned OFF.

In addition, the directional lights change depending on the type of scene.

3. On the CommandManager, click **Render Tools > Edit Scene**.
4. On the Task pane, click **Scenes > Studio Scenes**, and select the **Reflective Floor Checkered** scene from the browser. Notice two more directional lights related to the selected scene.

5. Rotate the model and notice that one light is fixed and the other rotates with the model.

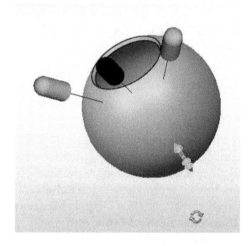

6. Click **OK** on the PropertyManager.
7. On the DisplayManager tree, right click on the **SOLIDWORKS Lights** folder and select **Add Directional Light**. A new directional light appears in the graphics window. The PropertyManager has three tabs: **Basic**, **SOLIDWORKS**, and **PhotoView 360**.

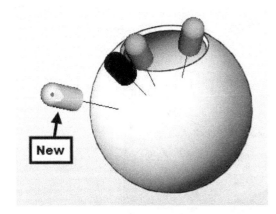

8. On the **Basic** tab, check the **Keep light when scene changes** option to retain the light for all the scenes.
9. In the **Light Position** section, drag the **Longitude** and **Latitude** draggers to change the position of the light (or) click and drag the light to define its position.
10. Uncheck the **Lock to model** option and rotate the model. Notice that the light is fixed as the model is rotated.
11. Check the **Lock to model** option and rotated the model. Notice that the light rotates along with the model.
12. Click the **SOLIDWORKS** tab on the PropertyManager. You can turn ON/OFF the light by checking the **On in SOLIDWORKS** option. You can also change the **Ambient**, **Brightness**, and **Specularity** of the light using **SOLIDWORKS Lighting** options.
13. Click the **PhotView 360** tab. You can turn ON/OFF the light while rendering by checking the **On in PhotoView 360** option.
14. Check the **Dynamic help** option and review the options on the **PhotoView 360** tab.
15. Click **OK** on the PropertyManager.

TUTORIAL 11 (Working with Point Lights)

A point light radiates lights in all directions. It can be used to add lightening effect to models such as torch lights.

1. Open the Tutorial 11 file.
2. Click the **DisplayManager** tab, and then click **View Scene, Lights, and Cameras**.
3. Right click on **SOLIDWORKS Lights** folder and select **Add Point Light**. A red dot appears in graphics window.

4. On the **View** toolbar, click **View Orientation > Four View**.
5. Make sure that the **Link Views** icon is activated on the **View Orientation** drop-down.
6. Click and drag the red dot as shown. You can also use the options in the **Light Position** section.

7. On the **Basic** tab, check the **Keep light when scene changes** option.
8. Click the **SOLIDWORKS** tab and adjust the Ambient, Brightness, and Specularity.
9. Click the **PhotoView 360** tab and check the **On in PhotoView 360** option.
10. Adjust the brightness, shadows, and fog.
11. Click **OK** on the PropertyManager.
12. On the **View** toolbar, click **View Orientation > Single View**.
13. Render the image as shown.

14. Save and close the file.

TUTORIAL 12 (Working with Spot Lights)

Spot lights are similar to the directional lights. However, they create brighter and sharp lights targeting a specific area.

1. Open the Tutorial 12 file.
2. Click the **DisplayManager** tab, and then click **View Scene, Lights, and Cameras** .
3. Right click on the **SOLIDWORKS Lights** folder and select **Add Spot Light**. A cone appears in graphics window.
4. On the **View** toolbar, click **View Orientation > Four View** .
5. Click and drag the red arrow as shown. You can also use the options in the **Light Position** section.

6. Drag the green circle of the cone to reduce its size.

7. Drag the red dot to set the target point of the spot light.

8. Check the **Keep light when scene changes** option.
9. Click the **PhotoView 360** tab and check the **On in PhotoView 360** option.
10. Increase the **Shadow quality** to 70 and click **OK**.
11. On the **View** toolbar, click **View Orientation > Single View** .
12. Change the **View Orientation** to **Trimetric**.
13. On the Task pane, click **Appearances, Scenes, and Decals** tab.

14. Click **Scenes > Basic Scenes**, and then drag the **Pitch Black** scene into the graphics window.
15. Render the image, as shown.

16. Save and close the file.

TUTORIAL 13 (Working with Sun Lights)

Sunlight in SOLIDWORKS represents the real-world sunlight and is controlled by the geographic location that you specify.

1. Open the Tutorial 13 file.
2. Click the **DisplayManager** tab, and then click **View Scene, Lights, and Cameras** .
3. Right click on **SOLIDWORKS Lights** folder and select **Add Sunlight**. The sun appears along with a compass.

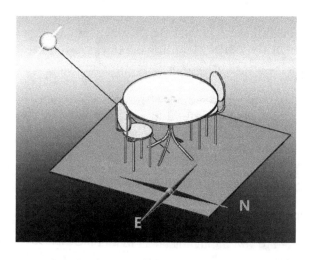

4. Select the right edge of the floor to define the north direction. You can also use a real compass to determine the north direction at your location, and then define it in SOLIDWORKS.

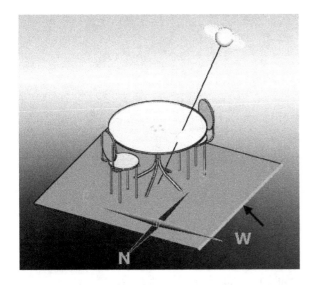

5. Click the **Reverse direction** button next to the **North direction** box. The position of the sun is changed, accordingly.

6. Select different locations from the Location drop-down and notice the position of the sun. In addition, the Time Zone is updated in the **Time zone from GMT** drop-down.

7. Under the **Location, Time, and Date** section, select **Location > Specify Location**.

8. Drag the **North Latitude** and **East Longitude** draggers to define the location. You can use a map as the reference, and enter values in the **North Latitude** and **East Longitude** boxes.

9. Select New York from City, NY from the Location drop-down.

10. Set the Date to 07-02-2015.

11. Set **Time of day** to 12:00. Notice that the **Information** section displays all the data related to the location. You can save this information in a file using the **Save to file** icon located at the bottom.

12. Click the **Advanced** tab and examine all the options with the **Dynamic help** option selected.

13. Click **OK** on the PropertyManager.

14. Click **Preview window** on the **Render Tools** tab and notice the shadows.

15. Close the Preview window.

16. In the DisplayManager tree, right click on **Sunlight** and select **Edit Sunlight**.

17. On the PropertyManager, change the **Location** to **Sydney**, and click **OK**.

18. Click **Preview window** on the **Render Tools** tab and notice the shadows.

19. Close the Preview window and file.

TUTORIAL 14 (Walk-through)

SOLIDWORKS Walk-through allows you to visually navigate through the design, and then create a video for the presentation purpose.

1. Open the Tutorial 14 file.

2. Click the **DisplayManager** tab, and then click **View Scene, Lights, and Cameras**.

3. Right click on **Walk-through** folder and select **Add Walk-through**. The PropertyManager appears.

Now, select a plane to define the vertical direction.

4. Make sure that the Top plane is selected. The vertical direction is defined normal to the selected plane/face.
5. Under the **Viewport Settings** section, set the **Viewing height** to 900. The viewing height is offset from the Top plane.
6. Expand the **Motion Constraints** section and select the spline, as shown. The motion path is defined.

7. Make sure that the **Turn avatar to follow paths** option is checked.
8. Click the **Start Walk-through** button on the PropertyManager.
9. Notice the **Walk-through Quick Start Instructions** and click **OK**.
10. Click the **Show/Hide Map** ⊞ icon on the Panel. The **Map View** window appears showing the position of the avatar.
11. Click the **Toggle Constraints** 🔓 icon on the Panel.
12. Click the **Lock to Constraint** 🔒 icon on the Panel. The avatar is locked to the path.
13. Click the **Set Home** 🏠 on the left side of the Panel. The start point of the path is set as home.

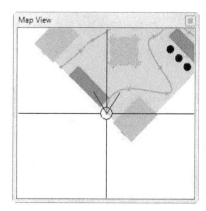

14. Press and hold the **Move Forward** arrow on the Panel. The avatar moves forward along the path. You can increase or decrease the avatar speed using the Rabbit and Turtle icons.

15. Click the **Go Home** 🏠 icon after reaching the endpoint of the path. The avatar is positioned at the start point.
16. Click the **Toggle Record** ⦿ icon on the Panel. The **Record** section appears.
17. Click the **Record** ⦿ icon in the **Record** section and navigate through the model.
18. Click **OK** on the Panel after reaching the end of the path.
19. On the PropertyManager, click **Play Recording** ▷ icon.
20. Close the **Record** panel after the avatar reaches the path end. If the video looks good, then proceed further to generate the video.
21. On the PropertyManager, **Generate Video** ▦ icon, type-in the name, specify the file type and location, and then click **Save**.
22. Select the **Video Compression** option and click **OK**.
23. Click **OK** on the PropertyManager.

TUTORIAL 15 (Decals)

SOLIDWORKS allows you to add images such as logos to your model by using the Decals option. Adding decals makes the rendered model look more realistic.

Adding the default Decals to the Model

1. Open the Tutorial 15 part file.
2. Click the DisplayManager tab, click the **View Decals** icon, and then click **Open Decal Library** button. You can also click the **Appearances, Scenes, and Decals** tab on the Task pane and select the **Decals** folder.
3. Click and drag the **Recycling** decal from the Task pane onto the model.

4. Click and drag the corner of the rectangle to change the size of the decal.
5. Click **OK** on the PropertyManager.

6. On the DisplayManager tab, expand the **Decals** tree, right click on **recycle**, and select **Delete**.

Creating your own Decals

1. Download the globe.jpg from the companion website.
2. On the CommandManager, click **Render Tools > Edit Decal**.
3. On the PropertyManager, click the **Browse** button.
4. Go to the location of the globe.jpg file and double-click on it.
5. On the PropertyManager, click the **Save Decal** button.
6. Click **Save** and SOLIDWORKS creates the *.p2d file.
7. On the SOLIDWORKS message, click **Yes** to add the location of the decal file to the Task Pane.

8. On the Task Pane, click the **Appearances, Scenes, and Decals** tab and expand the **Decals** folder. Notice the new folder added to the **Decals** folder.
9. Click on the new folder and notice the Decal in the lower portion of the Task Pane.
10. Select the globe decal from the Task Pane.
11. Select the outer surface of the model.

12. Click the **Mapping** tab on the PropertyManager. The options available on this tab are similar to that available on the **Mapping** tab of the texture PropertyManager.
13. Set the **Mapping** type to **Label**.
14. In the **Size/Orientation** section, change the **Rotation** value to **90** degrees.
15. Set the **Width** value to 50.
16. Use the Horizontal Location and Vertical Location draggers to position the decal properly.

17. Click the **Illumination** tab and check the **Use underlying appearance** option.
18. Click the **Image** tab on the PropertyManager.
19. Under the **Mask Image** section, select the **Selective color mask** option.
20. Click the **Pick color** icon.
21. Go to the **Decal Preview** section and select the white color from the preview image. The color is displayed in the **Selected colors** section and removed from the decal. You can remove it from

the **Selected colors** section by selecting and clicking the **Remove color** button.

22. Click **OK** on the PropertyManager.

23. Save and close file.

Index

www.ingramcontent.com/pod-product-compliance
Lightning Source LLC
LaVergne TN
LVHW060138070326
832902LV00018B/2849